Storms
Inland Sea

Storms of the Inland Sea

Poems of Alzheimer's and Dementia Caregiving

Edited by Margaret Stawowy and Jim Cokas

SHANTI ARTS PUBLISHING
BRUNSWICK, MAINE

Storms of the Inland Sea

Poems of Alzheimer's and Dementia Caregiving

Published by Shanti Arts Publishing
Designed by Shanti Arts Designs

Cover image is a compilation of images by
Johannes Plenio and Sascha Thiele, both on pexels.com.

Shanti Arts LLC
193 Hillside Road
Brunswick, Maine 04011
shantiarts.com

Printed in the United States of America

ISBN: 978-1-956056-40-2 (softcover)

Library of Congress Control Number: 2022939914

My deepest gratitude goes to Joann Cokas, my stepmother. My father's greatest love and advocate, she carried us all with strength and grace through those trying years.

—Jim Cokas

To my mother, Doris Stawowy, for, well, just about everything. This is for you, Mom!

—Margaret Stawowy

CONTENTS

EVENING GRAY

RED SKY IN THE MORNING

RING AROUND THE MOON

WALK ON WATER

SALVAGE

SALT

SWEET AND BLUE

Foreword

> There are only four kinds of people in the world: those who have been caregivers, those who are currently caregivers, those who will be caregivers, and those who will need caregivers.
> —Rosalynn Carter

For many, becoming a caregiver of someone with Alzheimer's or dementia entails a radical metamorphosis. It forces us to give up the luxury of viewing death and decline as an abstract concept and, instead, brings us face-to-face with its inevitability in a way that intellectualizing never can. Caregiving requires that we give ourselves over to a monumental task with a bleak outcome. To paraphrase the words of poet Mariana Mcdonald, we must submit to impossible thirty-hour days inside hundred-day weeks.

In my case, when my mother first showed signs of dementia, I was in denial. I rationalized that she was experiencing a temporary lapse that would soon pass, and life would go back to normal. Then in a defining moment (to which most caregivers can relate), I understood that "normal" was gone for good. Witnessing my mother's fear and helplessness, a shift occurred within, forcing me to deconstruct and reconstruct a new mindset. I had to give myself over to a chrysalis-like transformation.

Science tells us that inside a chrysalis, the caterpillar releases enzymes that break down the creature's very body to a liquidy substance. Yet in this primordial soup, cells are ready to unlock, grow, and metamorphose in a process nearly mythological in scope.

A similar evolution occurred in me, as it does to all dementia and Alzheimer's caregivers. But just as butterflies struggle to survive in nature, so do caregivers—from burnout, financial worries, loneliness, loss of loved ones as we once knew them, hard choices, and sadly, the judgment of others. That's only the start. Yes, we're answering a higher call to serve with as much grace, forbearance, and love as we can muster, but often at the expense of our own health and wellbeing.

My project partner, graphic artist and poet Jim Cokas, also contributed hands-on caregiving for his father who suffered from Alzheimer's. He resigned from a tenure-track teaching position to assist his stepmother, who could not handle the mounting tasks alone. While sharing our poems and his artwork, Jim wondered how many others were writing poems about dementia and Alzheimer's caregiving experiences. After research, I learned that while there were anthologies on the topic, none concentrated on the caregiving aspect through poetry.

In curating this collection of work, Jim and I wished we'd had poems such as these to carry us through difficult days of change and coping. We thank the poets in this anthology for sharing their experiences in powerful, insightful work. As Marc Harshman demonstrates in his poem "Inland Sea," caregivers learn to weather the storms of providing care, both practical and emotional, and to navigate those seas, our own and those of our loved ones.

Consider this anthology as a map, a guide to a place of transformation.

Margaret Stawowy
The Chrysalis Project

EVENING GRAY

ALZHEIMER DEFINITION

—after Alois Alzheimer (1864–1915), German neurologist

(altz hi - m rz) n. 1. Gradual sunset of memory. 2. A failure of
equations. 3. The abolition of space. 4. The abolition of time.
5. The dissolution of objects. 6. An unrecognizable silence.
7. Evaporated milk. 8. A blank stare. 9. An invasion of silence.
10. Speech no longer acts as protester. 11. A cloak of nothing known
or unknown. 12. The banishment of learning. 13. The disappearance
of all childhood riddles. 14. The dissolution of brain cells.

LOSING ANITA

You don't remember You cried
Come quick!

The blankets were falling from the trees

Rose-colored Gold-colored
Aqua Maroon

Blowing into Tumbling into
You into Me into

Muck-covered gloom

You kept pleading *Remember when?*
Will we ever again?

Wake into Spring into
Me into You into

Rose-colored Gold-colored
Aqua Maroon

A DARKNESS

There was nothing I could do to stop it

No way to stop the pull of death
The thick sheets of
forgetfulness
The mangled neurons
Tattered thoughts
The conquered lands of tyrant plaque

I could not stop the conquest

Nor could I hold back death
Put forth firm brakes
to say
Just once   just now   remember

In my desperation
I could not speed death
Ask haste
against a plodding misery
A thirty-hour day that lived
inside a week of
hundred-days

I could not do it

No matter what my strategy
Hope   pray   deny   despise
I was nothing next to it

All my courage paled
My valor sighed
against its vibrant force

I'd look into those eyes that once
were food and light to me
And saw instead
a darkness
terrible
and complete

There was nothing I could do to stop it

Brain Tangle

in terms ...
stiff as starched lab coats,
I'm told of a disease
resulting in babble language,
stammering, skipping words.
in ways ...
incomprehensible as the stars,
I strain to sort medical lingo,
cerebral falter, vascular stiffening,
white, sticky plaque.
my mind ...
primal and perplexed,
envisions serpents
tortuously entwined
injecting venom in the brain.
in the background ...
I hear stuttering,
beginning, pausing, stuttering again,
a botched script,
a theatrical performance.
what I know ...
I, too, am in this play,
a foreign actor
pressing the warmth of my palms
to the face I love.

CLOSE UP

Like a print creased from age,
flecks falling from the cracks,
we lost parts of her,

faded
a year at a time,
a month at a time,
a day at a time.

Some would have it
that a painting
is more true to reality
than is a photograph,
that it captures
a vibrancy,
a character,
a photo cannot.

I would argue
a photograph
is more true to reality,
no matter how
well-cared for,
with age
a photo fades,
loses its acuity
and color.

Paul Sohar

Remembering *Grossmutter*

Grandma is not going to the Black Church of Brasov
today. Not because Transylvania is a bit too far from here.
Mother managed to talk her out of it.

"*Schwarze Kirche* is closed today," she said. "Why don't
you just sit here and read a magazine." And she went off
to work, leaving me with Grandma in the quiet living room.

Grandma behaves herself, sitting straight like a lady, carefully
turning the pages of the magazine. I'm slumped down over a heavy
tome on dialectical materialism. Exams are coming up soon.

The needlepoint flowers of the upholstery are the loudest thing for
some time. Suddenly Grandma's voice breaks the silence like
a needlepoint flower dropping a petal.

"And you, sir," she speaks to me without taking
her glasses off, "may I ask who you might be?"

She looks as proper and polite as the porcelain vase on the coffee
table and the chintz curtain in the sunshine pouring in.

"Your grandson," I answer just as politely or perhaps because
I can't think of anything more reassuring to say.

"Sir," now her voice sharpens like a needle, "this is not my idea
of a joke. I think I'll go home."

"It's dangerous in the streets," I hasten to stop her. "Turkish cavalry
troops have invaded the city."

"The Turks?" she asks, sitting down in surprise. "Not the Russians?"

The dialectics of silence. I recall her keeping a tidy household and
slicing the bread a year or two earlier saying: *Ein stück ist ein stück.*

24

SHAKER

I have seen hen-scratched letters in the snow,
the ghost of a quail's tail feathers
like a sentence in the frost
that covers November's toppled grass,
I have seen hundreds of hand impressions
in the last slab of cement
on a walkway before the porch step
as if those childish fingers and palms were remarks
that could tell the story of the house
when things were happy there.
I've seen the drawn footprints of carpenters
in the sawdust that start apart like parentheses,
but as the day's drifts draw closer
drag into one long slur.
And I've heard the Parkinson's Morse code-tapping toes
of my father searching for the planks
of the floor I take for granted
like ellipses I can figure out,
a trick played by the disease
that makes him a Shaker, he says.
He begins to tell a memory
but says it's like a horse in a pen
and there's a padlock on the gate.

This morning a frost hardens,
and a varied thrush hops back and forth
hoping to find food in its footprint,
to scuff frost and make the ground pop up
a seed for its beak, but the frost
does not abrade. I listen, search
for my father in the spaces
of the stories he can't tell.

PINE CAKE

I ask what she sees, my constant question,
nudging her to use what few words
she has left. She studies the photograph
of me holding a cake crowned with a cluster
of candles: pink, yellow, green, blue.
Pine cake, she says, certain, and I reply,
Yes, a pound cake, not to correct
but to jar memory. I ask how she would
make one. Blank stare, though I remember
the stained page of her first cookbook,
its dark green paper cover, a collection
titled Ladies' Best Recipes from the radio station
in my father's hometown. Remember
the cake's scent sweetening even the bedrooms,
the taste when the first cooled bite arrived
moist and crumbly in my mouth. I name
the ingredients: a pound of flour, butter, sugar,
a cup of milk, six eggs. She shakes her head
no, as if that can't be right. No longer in need
of measurements, temperature, timing,
she's focused on what sparkles and shines,
the forest of candles flickering.

WORD SEARCH

She and I search
for one word
then another,
each hidden
in plain sight
among a diaspora
of words and letters.
Her pencil hovers
over the page
like a small
drone, hesitating
momentarily
over t-e-a.
I hold my breath,
but she moves on,
her mind unable
to connect these
three small symbols
to the white china cup
on the table beside her,
steam rising
from the dark liquid.
Her hand drops
down a row,
determined to locate
the elusive word.
I exhale.

Earl Grey

Mom does not remember
Earl Grey tea. That she prefers it.
That she loves it. No sugar. Just plain.
Don't ruin it with lemon. God forbid milk.

For all she knows, Earl Grey is a fine gentleman
riding from his castle in the English countryside,
galloping on his well-groomed steed. He halts
by the rocky brook to adjust his fine felt hat.

Mom, 93. My reminders, steady fuel, stoke
the furnace of her runaway locomotive.
But Mom, you love Earl Grey, your favorite!
Really? I do? Well, okay. If you say so.

Consider Earl Grey, Mom's former sixth-grader
who threatened to kill himself, ran from class,
apprehended by police on the 59th Street bridge.
That—she claims, shortened her life by a year.

Perhaps Earl Grey—no, he couldn't be an uncle.
It's rare to find a Jewish uncle named Earl Grey,
especially if said uncle debarked to Ellis Island
from a hell-hole shtetl in Eastern Europe.

The copper kettle shrieks. Mom unaware.
I pour steaming tea and fill our porcelain cups
with disbelief. Kitchen table. We sit before
a plate of scones, eat. Mom smiles. We sleep.

Pamela Peté

LEAVING HERE

back   to the beginning
as the present moves
so swiftly   she can't
take hold   and she
tries   memory's
tail   she can almost
touch   it moves just
out of reach   thin
vaporous   like a
ghost   she is not sure
was there   but is almost
sure   she can see it
don't you?

she can't share
no one understands
and you can't tell
her   she just ate
she would know
if she ate   after all
_i'm not crazy   do you
think i'm crazy?_

_where are we going now?
you just told me that
didn't you?
how many times?
how many days?
every day   i don't
go to the same place
i have never been_

here before   i have

never seen this doctor
before   don't live
here   haven't seen you
in a long time

what happened
to my tooth?

i don't want   to go back
love hurts   i'm afraid
afraid of what?   *i*
don't know   i'm just
afraid   you just
don't understand
you are strong   and
i'm   i'm not—like
you   i'm sorry   thank
you for putting up
with me   thank you
for taking me   thank
you   a thousand times
thank you

what are your goals?
let me get back to you
is there anything you
want to do?
let me get back to you
what do you want to eat?
what do you want to eat?
do you want dessert?
what kind of ice cream

do you like?   *i don't know*

what do you know? *i*

don't know anything
what do you want?
i don't want anything
well   i want a car
where will you go?   i
don't know
why do you want a car?
don't know
i have to go now
i'll be back tomorrow
okay   i'll miss you
remind me

what's your name?

TIMELESS

He lived in a sleepy town, an end of the road kind of place
you by-pass trying to get somewhere else, Timeless.

He liked its quiet: no trucks rumbling down Main Street,
no planes cruising overhead and no Wi-Fi.

He hardly heard from his brothers. They didn't know his address
or his phone in Timeless. He hadn't told them. Older. They were older.

And now he was the oldest, people telling him they hoped to be as fit
when they hit their eighties. When they said things like that he
    turned his back

and re-entered Timeless. In the morning, there was day.
The bedroom slowly filled with light; the dark escaped.

He was in his bed. He had slept. So it was day. But what day?
Once days flowed in orderly progression: stately Sunday,

hectic Monday and so forth. Then he moved to Timeless
and had to tolerate his wife telling him today was Tuesday

but Timeless resisted Tuesday, that crass intruder. Problems arose:
without Tuesday was it too soon to leave for the game on Sunday?

Don't let them think he'd forgotten. Better get ready now.
Now is putting on his coat, finding his favorite cap, his new black gloves.

They were as new as yesterday: that darkness he had slept through
when he woke up this morning.

Tired, he drifts into sleep, his head sinking down toward his shoulder
so the now would go away. He'll simply close his eyes and shut it out

and come back home to Timeless.

SOPHIE

shuffles in the hall in her slippers.
She speaks to herself in Polish

and in English. She asks you the time
and what is for breakfast, for lunch,

and for dinner. She asks you
how you are and rarely steps outside.

Years of psychiatric drugs
have made her tongue stick out.

Even after her single mastectomy,
she still keeps her money

tied in a roll around her neck
in the cleavage beneath her housecoat.

She makes sense of the world.
Sometimes she even sings.

NUISANCE

She tells me, *"It's a nuisance, all a nuisance."*
I ask, "What's a nuisance?"
"Everything's a nuisance," she replies,
using the few words remaining
in her muddled mind.

Librarian days behind her,
English Lit vocabulary gone,
she cannot write nor even sign her name.
She has nothing left to say but
"Nuisance" as a regular refrain
to express frustration at the loss
of independence, memory,
and even thought.

She never cursed and still does not,
but now the one word *"Nuisance,"*
spewed forth with venom and disgust,
says everything that she cannot.

"It's all a nuisance."

I agree.

DEMENTIA INTRIGUE

It grew up about her
like moss overtaking stones around a pond:
forgetfulness, increasing erasure of events,
an odd absentmindedness she experienced as fascinating,
until she found the hole in her consciousness frightening.

When her son mentioned the rosebush
that once graced their backyard's center,
her mind and her face went blank—
until she pretended to remember.
She wondered if he knew
she couldn't retrieve the sense of smell.
Taste was something she failed to locate
anywhere in her mouth's mysterious flesh.

When her daughter swung by on Memorial Day
and fifteen minutes after letting her in
she didn't recall her daughter entering the house,
her daughter gave her a look that murmured
compassion, but bellowed alarm.

It grew up around her
like cattails overwhelming a ditch,
until her passageways, her escapes
felt cluttered, even clogged,
until she didn't recognize noon.
Thought it was midnight.

BEREFT

My father has misplaced his children.
At ninety-two, he asks my brother
Where do you live?
Are you on the East Coast
or is that your sister?
He dozes and nods.
It is late December
and Christmas is over.

He wakes from his nap.
I ask him how he is.
I don't feel like I used to, he says.
I know I've been here before
but I can't remember this house.
Thirty years of visits
evaporate like so much rainwater.

The doctor says
that my father is healthy
his pulse is steady and strong.
My father's heart of leather
weathered as it is
beats on.

My Dad Loves Shrimp

Should I tell my Dad
his dead brother, Bob,
is not coming to lunch?

I'm treating my Dad to
a giant seafood dish,
a plate of jumbo shrimp.

Dad is grinning, looking
at his plate and saying,
"Tell Bob to come over
when he comes in."

Should I tell Dad
Bob died a long time ago
or Bob will find us
after we go to Mrs. Fields?

David M. Parsons

THEY

   —for Harry Dazey

Now that we know that Harry has Alzheimer's,
we catch ourselves wondering out loud

about our own memories, searching
for that small void in our understanding

of time's continuum. This cruel wound
that delicately as some evil surgeon unseals

the mute gray bindings that hold
ineffably the inventory of a life

stuns us again and again with horrific wonder,
leaving us with facial expressions, not unlike his

as he turns his bent spade, again and again,
like some blind farmer through

the rough weed-filled furrows
of recollection and recognition.

At the Garden Café, Ruth stately still,
rotely asks him in that wifely way:

Would you like tea or coffee, Harry?
Harry, do you want tea ... or coffee?

... then the realization... *oh... oh, give him tea.*
An acquaintance happens by the table,

and Ruth graciously, dutifully introduces her
to Harry, who, as always, smiles affably

and responds, *I am not really here,*
you know. Later, I accompany him

to the men's room, where he becomes confused
and begins to wash his hands before entering

the small dark stall with its endless
roll of blank white sheets of paper.

Standing before the sink, he stares
with what appears to be rapt erudition into the mirror

and whispers in that familiar, gentle fatherly tone,
He wants to come back you know; he wants to come back

and they—they won't let him.

THE CHORE

Once he built a house,
but now it's hard for him
to make a sandwich,
and so I try to think
of tasks that he can do.

The dishes he can wash
for me to rewash later
if I can find them when
he puts them, wet, away.

Most days he naps
after staying up at night,
or he stares at the TV set
with no new news.

Not long ago, he saw
a stray dog in our yard,
and so he followed it
down the road until
what wasn't there
had disappeared.

Ann Farley

ON THE SUNSET, EASTBOUND

We leave earlier than necessary
to go to the neurologist's office.
I lie about the appointment time,
because nothing slows an elderly person
like being rushed.

We snake the sloping curves
to the tunnel into Portland, traffic thick
but moving, until, abruptly, it isn't.
We stop, and I calculate the distance left,
the chances of finding parking near an elevator,
the hallways we need to walk,
how often he might shuffle to a stop
to ask a question
or gaze out a window.

Time trickles while we sit
like rocks in a river.
I am careful not to fidget or sigh.
But he leans forward,
examines the cars, the hillsides,
the tall trees, the downward twist of the road.
Then he focuses on me. His eyebrows arch.
He says, *This is good.*
I know this place.

Search Party

—for Jack Lloyd

Maybe he watched the whole time
and thought it's good for you
to get together like this
and let all your umbrellas bloom.

Or because he was so emptied
of words thought nothing
we could wrap a story around.
The river bent beside us
without shining, all bloat
and roughed-up pewter.

Days shed into nights like wet smoke.
In alley after alley faces stared
into the pokehole of the flashlight.
It didn't matter that any one of them
could have been God.
We were not looking for God.

Maybe he turned the corner
without thinking: The way back
is to undo what I have just done.
He found tracks, the regular ties.
Trains had always taken him home.
Shivering weeds might not strike him
as a clue. Drops slipped from clouds
the way words fell from him.

The lull of walking. He moved
uninflected through wet air deepening
his way into the dark field. What was left
to know? He came to the world wordless—

one way to be lost in the heart
of things. Everything
breathed for him—the night,
the searchers, his wet shoes.

Grasses bent down, offered themselves.
Storm-slashed willows meshed
a draggled room for him. Wind
threading through soothed:
Lie down ... lie down here,
man whose name
is flying away.

Pamela Peté

MIND ERASURE

it's not right i know
to grieve over someone
that is still here

not holding anything
you must grip   to let go
as she
slowly   lets go
let's   go

and i know it's not right
to cry myself   for myself

not her   although it's her
plight   and so selfish i
feel it's not me that
can't remember
remember only yesteryear

standing still and peeing
not seeing the toilet right
there   right there

there   and feeling bad   and
sad   and mad that she can't

remember
      that she can't remember

but i remember
    and i'm not ready
       for her to go
         not ready
           not while i'm
still here

44

LEARNED AT LAST NIGHT'S LECTURE ON DEMENTIA

My mother's brain, ink-dark
with dying cells, pocked with holes.
We say someone's not firing on all cylinders,
not knowing it's true, that sick cells
fire, don't fire, don't fire, fire,
launch messages. into.   the dark

    spaces.
where. memory.   once

                lived.

I've found shells on the beach
riddled with pin-sized punctures,
maple leaves reduced to lace skeletons.
It's not that what's missing
had no importance.
Only that there's beauty still
in what remains.

ALZHEIMER'S FOR BEGINNERS

All your life
you've collected antiques
and now you are one.

You've forgotten
your daughter's name
and call her "Mother."

Your son, you call "Father."
(He's not amused.)

You brush your white hair
with your red toothbrush,
and, on occasion, wear
your underclothes on top
of outer ones, ready for
TV's Maidenform ads or
Playboy for octogenarians.

You cannot tie your shoes,
zip zippers, or snap snaps.
You cannot make your bed,
set a table,
or write your own name,

but you laugh at jokes,
listen to music,
enjoy good food,
and read, and re-read,
and re-read (out loud)
short notes from old friends.

You stare at sunsets,
praising each
and calling us
to come and see.

Sometimes we do,
and sometimes we don't,
thinking we have more
important things to do,
although I can't remember what.

RED SKY IN THE MORNING

My Mother Lives at Ocean House

My mother's eyes,
red-rimmed, rheumy,
scuttle like tiny sea crabs
sideways. She is blind.
I read to her, sing.
There has been a sea change
in my mother.

What was sound in my mother
is gone now. Close to her window
an ocean roars. In the shells of her ears,
waves are a bare whisper. I question her.
Where has she been? She leans toward me,
struggling. Her mouth opens, clamps shut.
What was sound in my mother
is gone now.

Outside, the ocean is rising.
I shore up words,
weave them together
in weedy strings,
I heave sibilance over
my mother's silence.
I pour
      words . . .
over her head . . .
like water.

I give her my eyes.
I give her my throat.
I give her the words
she couldn't utter.

SWIMMING IN THE RAIN

With my hands on her still strong shoulders,
I steer my mother
to the discount rack,
so she won't complain
about the prices.
The salesgirl comes over,
wearing an Oregon Ducks T-shirt,
her smartphone squeezed
into the back pocket
of her rhinestone jeans.
Cracking her gum, she asks
my mother in slow motion,
CAN-I-HELP-YOU?
My mother is slow as rain,
a creaky, twisted
bicycle chain.
Back at the car, she lifts
the black bathing suit
and folds it neatly on her lap.
"I look like a fat seal in that thing,"
she says, and I tell her,
"And I'm a seagull
crashing into the surf."
It's been raining
for hours
both of us swimming now
in uncharted waters.

INLAND SEA

She did not want me to see her riding her sad whales
   through the green waves.
She told me this as I helped her sop up the mess.
The bathtub had overflowed again.
It was hard to understand, and I had lots of questions.
Soon, though, Mother wasn't listening.
It happened a lot. Not listening.
Tidal waves of water and questions.
Someone told me that my father was leaving her.
He is always leaving, I say.
I love you, I tell her, just in case.
Still, she isn't listening,
   despite the empty room, the dry floor.
I say those words again, and again:
   I love…
Her hair is night-black with a silver sweep
   where the moon's knife once slashed it.
Perhaps she had dreams bigger than her heart could manage.
I decided it was funny how Father could have been
   the right man but at the wrong time.
Not tragic or bad, but *funny.*
I was big on love in those days; *funny* allowed me to love him, too.
And I came to learn that that *wrong time* provided my only passage here.
Still, I would have wished better things for her.
Bankruptcy, alcohol, violent silences stood always between them
   and in front of me
   all these years
   just waiting
   for me
   to find my way round.
I keep repeating what I'd said.
She continues to sit in the bath.
The listening has been over a long time now.

Still, I'm patient, have my sponge ready,
   and those words,
   those words, those
   I always have,
   ready, too, to have them
   returned.

THE BATH

The tub fills inch by inch,
as I kneel beside it, trail my fingers

in the bright braid of water.
Mom perches on the toilet seat,

entranced by the ritual until
she realizes the bath's for her.

Oh no, she says, drawing her
three layers of shirts to her chest,

crossing her arms and legs.
Oh no, I couldn't, she repeats,

brow furrowing, that look I now
recognize like an approaching squall.

I abandon reason, the hygiene argument,
promise a Hershey's bar, if she will just,

please, take off her clothes. *Oh no,*
she repeats, her voice rising.

Meanwhile, the water is cooling.
I strip off my clothes, step into it,

let the warm water take me
completely, slipping down until

only my face shines up, a moon mask.
Mom stays with me, interested now

in this turn of events. I sit up.
Will you wash my back, Mom?

So much gone, but let this
still be there. She bends over

to dip the washcloth in the still
warm water, squeezes it,

lets it dribble down my back,
leans over to rub the butter pat

of soap, swiping each armpit,
then rinses off the suds with long

practiced strokes. I turn around
to thank her, catch her smiling,

lips pursed, humming,
still a mother with a daughter

whose back needs washing.

AHAB

I've read *Moby-Dick*,
so many times I no longer
discuss it in public.
I'll try a pagan friend,
thought I, since Christian
kindness has proved but
hollow courtesy. Or,
The Whaleship was my
Yale college and my Harvard.
But I saw only
The Limits of Knowledge.
The Problem of Evil.
Multitudinous meanings
and symbols to be correlated
on the *Pequod's* deck.

My mother had a stroke.
The blood-tide
washing from her memory,
my father, my sister
and me. When my anger
surfaced, I sat up in bed.
Ahab and I had finally
met. His loss was mine.
Compassion had
a foot in the door.

DRUGGING MY MOTHER

My hands shook when I took the bag of drugs
delivered that night. The moon was red.
My mother's gut clenched, bred an infection,
dispersed invasive seeds of rage.
In her brain, a chainsaw shredded reason
to ribbons, incited limbs to insurrection.
Hospice gave clear directions: *Don't worry*
about tomorrow today. But that day,
electrons in her head split atomic bonds
of mother/daughter. I could hide knives, scissors,
but not my fear, which she could smell clearly.
Lorazepam, Seroquel, haloperidol.
I ferried the dark waters of my mother.
Tossed futile chemicals into her currents.

REMNANTS

My mother's eyes close, but her fingers
keep tracking across the page,
her lips moving as she turns
the pages backwards. When I ask her
what she's doing, she says,
I'm thinking what I'm going to do.
Her finger points to a circled word:
We've got something like this
and we couldn't figure it out.
As I jot down the sentence, noting
it's half in the present, half
in the past, she stares at my hand.
I don't have a pencil.
I dig in my bag, find notepad
and pen. *Now what am I going to do?*
Her eyelids flutter, the pen falls
from her hand. The question hangs
like laundry left on the line
long after it's dry.

MOTHER MATH

She'll tell you herself
she was never good at math,
the x's and y's jumping around
her day as if she were trying
to read without glasses.

In the dark she dresses:
blue-striped blouse, tan slacks,
new shoes with Velcro straps.
So far the numbers add up, but now
a missing purse—she put it on the table
last night—and a missing person,
her son-in-law, who should be here
to take her to the dentist.
At 4 am she calls her daughter.

Next month?
That can't be right.
Her daughter tells her to write
plans for the day in a notebook.
She can't find the notebook,
or the book she needs to return
to the library, or the library.
Such a lovely collection lost,
one more unsolved equation.

MANNERS

Always a lady, she compliments
the hospital bed and its ups and downs,
the gray-mashed beans, the flavorless broth,
and me, who knows "so very much" about
myself, "an excellent researcher" to have discovered
her writer daughter, who also, coincidentally,
is named my name, which she's always loved.
Don't I love it, too?

"Such a small world," she murmurs
before asking me to please
pass the No-Salt salt.

She shivers. I help her tug
the thin cover up evenly to her chin.
When my sister returns to the room
with a newly warmed blanket
and the nurse she has gone to fetch,
then sits with me again at the bedrail,
my polite mother asks, "Have you met
my other daughter? The beautiful one?"
"Yes," I nod. "She's lovely."

When her mind and body
again thrash violently
and "for her own protection" (the aides explain)
they strap her into a straightjacket,
my mother pleads with us to find
her daughters, who "are always happy to help."
"Thank you so much," she smiles,
before glaring at us suddenly
with someone else's impolite eyes.

Always a lady, my mother
does not know that she's not
who she is at the moment,
swearing at the nurses she thinks
are strangling her, at the intern
who, surely, has stolen her car,
the one we will take away
"for her own protection,"
after the MRI and CAT scan,
after the final diagnosis: common
infection that hijacked her brain
temporarily, which she will not remember
when she returns to her polite small talk,
to the well-mannered children she recognizes
and calls by name, the names she's always loved.
Don't we love them, too?

(I Lost My Child)

i lost my child
have you seen her
she's seven
and sweetly simple
or maybe three
just a willful toddler
or she could be thirteen
so impulsive
she used to be eighty-three
then she got lost
and i've been looking ever since
now i'm caught in the nowhere
between suspended grief
and contrived hope
knowing in my heart she's alive
somewhere
alone and frightened
and looking for me
but i can't find her
i lost my child
i lose her every day
and i can't find my mother

In Mid-Afternoon

In mid-afternoon, a woman bends over her nightstand to pick up the telephone receiver. She lifts it to her ear, hears worry in her grown daughter's voice. "Don't forget," she says, "it takes me a long time to walk through the house to answer the phone." She doesn't tell her daughter, maybe she has already forgotten, she was still in bed. The woman is annoyed by the long stalls in her own speech and the tangled path to remembering. Faces belonging to her daughter and sons float to the surface of her mind, like photographs developed out of sequence from a roll of film shot over a lifetime. Her children today, her children as infants, her children leaving home, her children older than she is now: Who are they? Who is she? "I love my children more than anything," she tells the person over the phone—yes, the person—her daughter. "But sometimes, you people need to back off so that I can put the box back together again, like on an assembly line." More than her own forgetfulness, she is annoyed by her children's talk. "I wish you all would stop asking me about my pills. Pills! Pills! Pills! I can't keep talking about this stuff," she says.

Outside her bedroom window, the stray cats mew for food.

"I do want to live with you, daughter," she says, "but first I need to—I need to feed the cats—let's just—oh, what was I going to say?—Let's just take one step at a time. I told that man—your brother—that I picture myself an old lady sitting on the porch in a rocking chair dispensing wisdom." Her daughter says something, then quickly apologizes. "What's that you say? Heaven help us! I'm not offended. I still have a sense of humor." Outside her bedroom window, there are as many roads as the pathways in her brain.

Who will feed her cats?

Michele Wolf

Miss Lake Hiawatha

I discovered the trophy, goddess of my mother's mythology—a golden
Winged figurine reaching heavenward, clasping a leafy, branched
Bouquet, the figure five inches tall atop the base—while clearing out
The layered dregs of the apartment. First my mother's mind
Had flickered, then the grid turned black in chunks. She would not
Bathe, could not recall what you had said the moment before, always
Kept a cigarette, her personal tiki torch, burning. The haze of smoke
Had morphed the walls from ivory to a mottled tan. Even the interior
Of the freezer had baked to tan. She soon needed twenty-four-hour
Surveillance, this raggedy woman, once a radiant presence
Whose full, flirty lips and ample, stark hazel eyes had made heads turn.

The miniature plaque on the wooden base reads, "L.H.C.C. 1950 Beauty."
She had said no to five marriage proposals before accepting my father's,
At nineteen. It was the champion bullying of her second husband,
Not the death of her first one, that destroyed her. "Why don't you ever
Take me on vacation?" she once asked, her mother and sister stationed
At the table to witness. "Because you're a stupid idiot," he replied.
After the divorce, she had to steal the beauty of everyone in the room,
To be the locus, the golden figurine. She perfected the art of having
A man sidle up to her in a bar, offer to light her cigarette, affirm
Her looks. Dating became a crusade, a career. What she never
Told us, what I learned from the newspaper folded up with the prize,
Was that she didn't win the contest. She was second runner-up.

The golden trophy is tiny, almost a toy. Upon entering old age,
Muscles atrophy. The scaffold of bones gets brittle and shrinks.
The entire figure gets reduced. In her final weeks, my pretty mother
Never ventured to speak. She sat in a wheelchair, under a coverlet,
Quivering, her hazel eyes cloudy, gazing through me, gazing out
At a space beyond. Did she know who I was? On my last visit, I knew
She grasped I was somebody kind. "Would you like me to hold
Your hand?" I asked. Quickly, she exhaled one soft syllable: "Yes."

Prayer for My Mother

Let every moment of every day
break upon her with the dazzle of
utter newness, and let her exult in it.

Let wonder rule: the sky more lovely
than she's ever seen, the birds that
come by the hundred to her feeder.

Let her forget that she does not
remember. Let her lose somehow
the torment of losing her mind.

Let there be insight in the one page that,
over and over for days, she reads
for the first time, never gets beyond.

Let the living past be vibrant in her
dreams each night, her mother, her brother
at her side, showering her with love.

Please let her eyes open in the morning
not to the despair of the lost at sea,
but to the sunlight sifting through

the leaves outside her window,
the solid sense that she is safe,
the familiar ground of home.

WHITE FLAG

And now I pretend
to pray—
my secret mourning,
secret even from myself.
Too soon to cry, she's still
smiling at me, still
finding the rhythm in Louis Prima,
still my mom.
Do I pray because I should have cried
sooner? I pray like a child
as if making a wish, as if tears
would be my surrender
to the wheelchair, her swollen hands,
the odd twist in her smile.
Mine is an ambiguous white flag
I raise for me, for her
when she waves goodbye.

THE HUNGRY

Over the phone most evenings, my mother tells me
she's cooked enough food for ten people: ham, roast,
always a chicken, with some assortment of side dishes,
sure to include overcooked canned green beans and iceberg lettuce.

I always ask who she expects to see at the table?
Who did she invite? Her answer, she can always find
hungry people, followed by the regular complaint,
when will I be there to help her eat this feast?

No one has shown up for a variety
of reasons: car won't start, flat tire, sick,
and my excuse is distance, 160 miles, one way.
She always acts surprised, sometimes asking

me where I live, though I've lived in the same house
for 40 years, and then more astounded that a round trip
from my house to hers and back takes 6 hours. She wants
to know if I'm married yet, which is another 40 years to reconcile.

Tomorrow the distance will be the same but feel farther.
In her kitchen, fired in hell, every pot and pan
scorched, unidentifiable remnants of a battlefield:
handles half-melted, metal bottoms warped by heat,

the defeated history of her falling asleep while cooking.
The guest list grows longer by the day, so much food to feed
hungry ghost battalions. And there's the frozen pizza
baked in its box waiting to be pulled from the oven.

Ring Leader

I'm yelling at my mother over the phone
the way she used to yell at me
fifty years ago in the kitchen
of another trailer, another house.

Wherever, whatever it was: something broken,
something not working,
something misplaced, it was
undeniable, without doubt, my fault.

Now she's caught me.
It's one of her final satisfactions,
that I'm no different from her as she enters
into a second childhood.

This is a bad movie, two senescent characters,
their anchor gray hair
backlit by a window, battling
for territory that's disappearing fast

as Arctic ice, knowing there's
nothing to be gained, defeat
everywhere: the polar bear gone,
the Arctic fox gone, the seal gone.

Nothing to hide and everywhere
to hide it. She can't talk on the telephone
and cook without dishing up
blackened oatmeal. She can't talk

on the cordless without tripping
on the basement steps. She can't talk
on the phone as the television broadcasts
to the neighborhood whatever it is

she's watching. I've repeated three times
what I've just said, each time increasing
the decibels of my voice, as I grip
the telephone like a pistol expecting

kickback. The shouting resumes.
She believes there's a conspiracy
to move her out of her house where she's lived
half a century, and I'm the ringleader.

AT 97

My mother
most days now
asks me if it's Tuesday
or January
earnest in her voice
and she stares at me
hoping she got it right
this time.
I tell her it's September
and we both laugh.
Years ago
I used to question
Mom and Dad
about the three of us
being more like friends
but she'd always just tell me
with a stern grin
to be good
and finish my dinner.
Secretly I longed to be
more like her
so I'd fit in
the way she did
sure of herself
no-nonsense
seemingly unafraid
of the dark or the future
and where life would ever take us.
She wanted a man for a son
but I only planned
to be
her little boy
so I could keep her
young and the same.

Sometimes I think
Mom's hands and fingers
surely have total recall
of everything she's done
all her work
organizing and putting away
keeping together
touching, caressing
pulling us close
or refusing to let go.
My mother taught me
how we pray
palm to palm, how we hold
a blue crayon, how to tie
my shoes
or sew a button
on an old shirt
and how we shape
then flatten
raw meat
to make a hamburger.
Today we mostly hold hands
and smile at each other.
Gratefully
mothers also teach us
how to talk
with our eyes
a physical Motherese
and this is what
keeps her nearby
wherever she might go
growing older
forgetting the how and why
becoming gray.

GOOD SON

When he visits his mother at dinner time
and helps with her feeding, they all tell him
what a good son he is

sometimes though, he wants to be a bad boy
and shove the food in her face, especially
when she spits out broccoli and clomps
her mouth shut wanting only ice cream

if he yells at her, she turns her head and stares
at nothing, goes rigid, moans, even when he calls
for staff, they don't help, just shrug, keep going

mother and son sit glaring at each other
as she gnashes her dentures until one
slight tear tries to begin a cry

a slow, sad, single tear runs down her cheek
and hangs dangling from her lightly
whiskered chin, a drop of rain, a fairy
fortune teller's globe, a tiny glass heart

there, there, he says, good son that he is
caring enough to lean in with a tissue
to pat the tear dry, and spoon in the ice cream
she opens her mouth to graciously receive.

THE MEMORY CARE PANTOUM

He thinks I'm his girlfriend
on the drive to the doctor when I hold his hand,
and the sun rips open a bank of clouds—
O I love you, father gushes out the open window.

On the drive to the doctor when I hold his hand,
a stilled raccoon bows beside the grey road.
O I love you, father gushes out the open window.
The week unwinds as we travel wide, wild lands.

Still, the raccoon bows beside the grey road.
He just keeps lying there and lying there, father says.
The weeks unwind as we travel wide, wild lands.
He once flew me home right through the heart of a storm.

He just keeps lying there and lying there. Father says
he thinks I'm his girlfriend.
He once flew me home right through the heart of a storm
and the sun ripped open a bank of clouds.

KNEELING

Her ankles.   Toes.   Her yellowing nails:
        groove   lunula   hallux.   I bend
to my basin.   Its warming pour, its
        attar of lavender . . .

Kneel: to unlace   the stiff shoes   to slip
        cuffed socks   roll up the slacks   flesh:
calves   indented. Cinctured.   Rough-
        reddened joints . . .

Her vessel   of days: its thirty-one thousand
        drops.   *Mother. Daughter . . .*The swelling
nights: who cradled my crown
        in her womb . . .

Who   in the darkened theatre   shed
        her shoes   barefoot   *Shall We Dance?*   Not
counting   edema: gather of waters.
        Her weeping . . .

I gather: her arch   her heel   her proud ankle
        once   slim as a wrist.   The twenty-six thin-
worn bones of the foot. Their intricate
        joinery. Journey . . .

You are my daughter?   Salt scrub. Infusion
        of bergamot. Not yet   translucent: her
thinning skin.   In the yielding   towel, cradle
        each instep . . .

Urge   the trapped fluid   back to the heart. . .
        Ginger and Fred. We showed off our steps
at the dance… where is your father? This
        synapse   also . . .

unmooring . . . tranced   she closes
        her lost eyes   and dreams   under skin steeped
in sun and aloe lotion   (who could not honor
        such rapture . . . ?)

Seized up   *ahhhh*   delight   she opens she
        strokes: her hand   my cheek. *You: my*
daughter. Such
                a good daughter.

WHAT DOESN'T CHANGE

My mother's wicked twinkle
when she laughs. How she goes,
Umm, uh, uh, umm, uh,
when she is worried
and will not say why.
If I could be inside
her brain, I'd know
how everything has changed—

collapsed tunnels light will never
see again, chattering mice
that gnaw the fragile walls
nearly away. That I name this
in metaphor
does not change
except when it does.
When what is, is. I make

the best of it. Paint her nails
with bright colors she loved,
comb her hair just enough
to leave the curls and laugh
when she laughs, because
it doesn't really matter what's
so funny now. My love for her
has changed. It used to

flow uneasily,
a moat with bridges
to be lowered and raised. Now
it is a river wide enough for barges.
Touching hands across, we float
downstream, heading for the same
destination, though she'll be first
to reach dry land.

PORTRAIT OF MY MOTHER AS A DRIED SUNFLOWER

The round shape of you
no longer round,
bent in on yourself
as if you are trying to find your way
back to the place you began.
You smell of dust
and still that scent
of only you.
I cannot see what you were
in what I have before me,
though in dreams you still stand
tallest in the field.
Every day a little
more of you
is gone. You are
beautiful.
You are so beautiful.
At the center,
a constellation of seeds
never planted.

GIFT

My father can't go to the forest
so I conjure one, pointing to a small
grove of trees in the park where we're sitting —

> *See over there, behind those trees*
> *that's where the trail begins*
> *we used to carry our packs up steep slopes*
> *to lakes full of trout and nap on*
> *granite slabs at the end of the day*
> *—remember?*

He smiles, shaking his head.
A flock of birds fly over, too fast
for him to notice, so I bring them to
his ear—cooing softly
hoping he'll remember the pigeons he
kept as a teenager and the joy he knew
releasing them to fly for a day.

Nearby a small boy sits in his
swing while his mother pushes him into
great arcs of joy. He smiles and waves
to my father, who knows to do the same.
He needs no help to remember what to do
how to respond, how to accept
a pure gesture.

Back from our trip to the park, I bend down
to adjust his wheelchair.
Feeling his hand
stroking my head
I stand up, surprised. He takes
my arm, stroking it over and over
then bringing it to his lips
in a soft
gentle
kiss.

ROOMMATES

my father Nick   is wheeling himself to his shared
room   in his deaf Silence   his blind Vision

he gropes for the hand of his roommate Don who
is not there   I wheel him   to the hospice room

where Don lies   alone   Don tells me   *I want*
to go back with Nick   I want to be with Nick

together they hold hands these elderly men veterans
of a world war   squeezing hands   back and forth

I watch   until   no squeezes

my father kisses Don's hand tells me he will wheel
himself   to the chapel   he wants to be alone

the next day   Dad's right eye droops his mouth puckers
food he has forgotten to swallow   spittle drools

from his mouth   I summon the nurse   we clean him
she whispers   *more small strokes*   *yes* I say *I know*

sorrow overcomes me   she touches   my shoulder
your father and Don   they were amazing roommates

she tells me   she found them last week   side by side
in wheelchairs   gazing   out the window   conversing

in parallel   dementias

CHANGELING

The Sidhe have given up on babies. Now they take our mothers.

She climbed the Wicklow Hills, called after a missing lamb, listened
for bleats as Dublin's lights danced to the east. She sings to herself now
in a language I do not understand.

I adjust her socks around her calves, secure the strap that holds her.

In a Rathmines flat, she waited for her older sister to come home
and add her coat onto the four the double bed already owned.
She looks at me, says her sister's name and grins.

I call her the childhood name she calls herself and take her hands.

Time is a series of flashes in a dark room where windows
are swollen shut and the wallpaper has let go, but the structure is sound—
her heart is strong. Had I not been here all along, I would not
        have known her.

I'm going to boil dinner for twelve in an eggshell to make sure she's mine.

RING AROUND THE MOON

Andrea Hollander

LIVING ROOM

In the cave of memory my father
crawls now, his small carbide light
fixed to his forehead, his kneepads
so worn from the journey they're barely
useful, but he adjusts them
again and again. Sometimes
he arches up, stands, reaches, measures
himself against the wayward height
of the ceiling, which in this part of the cave
is at best uneven. He often hits his head.
Other times he suddenly
stoops, winces, calls out a name,
sometimes the pet name he had
for my long-dead mother
or the name he called his own.

That's when my stepmother tries
to call him back. *Honeyman*, she says,
one hand on his cheek, the other
his shoulder, settling him
into the one chair he sometimes stays in.

There are days she discovers him
curled beneath the baby grand,
and she's learned to lie down with him.
I am here, she says, her body caved
against this man who every day
deserts her. *Bats,* he says, or maybe,
field glasses. Perhaps he's back
in France, 1944, she doesn't know.
But soon he's up again on his knees,
shushing her, checking his headlamp,

adjusting his kneepads, and she rises
to her own knees, she doesn't know
what else to do, the two of them
explorers, one whose thinning
pin of light leads them, making
their slow way through this room
named for the living.

HE SAYS MY MOTHER'S NAME

Our old home rang with choruses of your name,
Darlene, Darlene. Those last few times visiting
in Great Falls, I heard it soon after I entered,
his voice from the living room asking when dinner
would be, where the cats were, sometimes
just saying *animal*, sometimes *cattle*, sometimes
what's its name? Night, you set the coffee maker
for 4 in the morning, so that when he woke,
he would find it waiting for him, so he wouldn't
worry. One morning when I was there, it didn't work,
so I assured him that I could make the coffee,
pour the grind into the filter, pour water,
press the button. When I opened the door
of the bedroom, he heard, began asking for you,
Darlene, Darlene, like the call of a bird in winter.
No, it is me, I said, knowing he was disappointed.
I was up early to pour some coffee and drive
into the dawn to the north side of the river
to startle light and antelope, mule deer
in the ravine who bounced out of my sight.
My brothers and I laughed about it, this persistent call,
your name, Darlene, should I put this in the dishwasher,
Darlene, how do I turn on the vacuum, Darlene,
where did the dishwasher go, where should
I put this milk? You stayed up with me
when he went to bed just after dinner, and he
did not say your name again, the house quiet
with cats lying on the TV table, on the rocking
chair, in the window seat, the silence practicing
for when he would be gone. I imagine now
what that sound meant to him, your name, how
at the end of those two sounds was that primal desire
to hear you respond, say, what do you need?
Just a second. I'll be right there. This duty
of love I will never understand. He says your name
from deep inside himself, and you say *yes* again.

OIL OF OLAY: AN APOSTROPHE

The wind scatters maple leaves
just beginning to curl in frost,
the color of ending and beginning,
of a moon pared down to a translucent
self. Any blunder you made cost
a litany of your faults
despite your years of servitude:
packing his lunches that were never
good enough, hearing that you
did not know how to do anything
right. The roast was tough,
the chicken undercooked,
and his Catholic mother, blind
from diabetes, kept a cleaner house
and baked a better pie, and *Jesus Christ,*
get to the point, nobody wants to hear
all of that—you do not even know
how to tell a story.

The last time I saw you alive,
you sat in the living room, an afghan
you knitted yourself—shades
of blue—draped across your narrow lap.
I looked into your hyacinth eyes.
Could you go get my lotion?
It's on top of my vanity. My hands
are so dry. I removed the bottle's
black top and poured a thin pink
line of *Oil of Olay.* It overflowed
onto your robe, which, Father hiss-spit,
he had *just washed it for the third*
time this week, goddamn it.
Then there was his obstinate
refusal of the certified nurse-assistants
who pressed the doorbell
three days in a row after I called

and arranged for their services.
Ding-dong, ding-dong,
the same two-toned song

that chimed rarely in my childhood:
Avon lady calling! Mrs. Donovan
smelling faintly of cigarettes and rum,
you politely leafing through the glossy
pages of a catalogue, ordering just one
tube of Briar-Rose-red lipstick—
that's all you needed right now.
The paper boy on his bicycle
collecting the monthly fee for his route,
or Miss Wheatley just stopping by
sometimes on her round-the-block
walk with her ancient, blind dog at dusk,
its eyes oblique moons of opal
in the bat-flutter of streetlights.

Father sat *real quiet-like in his favorite
chair,* waiting for them to disappear,
he told me later, the same strategy
he uses when Jehovah Witnesses
tap tap tap politely on the door,
their silhouettes tilted with the weight
of briefcases filled with brochures
promising heaven on earth.
He did not want any strangers
in his house. I think I was five
the first time I heard this diatribe.
This was his castle and he was king,
a line from Tennessee Williams
he never read but saw on the black
and white RCA: Marlon Brando
in all his rain-soaked machismo
yelling up to an empty window
in his whiny, baby voice.

Decades ago, home
from college during winter break,
while we sat at the dining room table,
the TV blaring football's instant replay,
magic chalk outlining strategies
of loss or gain, you asked me about
my classes. He narrowed his eyes
to a dark line of utter disdain.
Think you're something
with all of that Shakespeare.
Now the king wanders like Lear
from room to room, trusting no one,
lost in his circumscribed ranch house
storm, frantic, unable to find his way
out of a wet paper bag without you.

The Last Love Poem for Jeff

You are my you
my only you
My Winnie the Pooh
my diddly doo.

Of all the animals in the zoo
I choose the ewe, I mean the you.
Of all the trees in Kalamazoo
I choose the yew, I mean the you.

Of all the letters old and new
I choose the u, I mean the you.
Of all the functions, f of u
I choose the identity, just plain you.

Ghosts say boo. Cows say moo.
But who says you?
Only you.

Dane Cervine

UNION

They were married, both stricken with Alzheimer's, living together in one room at Harbor Hills. They would constantly try on clothes—he a skirt, she his shirt. Often his pants would end up on her arms; her shoes fit snugly over both his hands. What tragic grace, at the end of life together—so determined to fit each inside the other.

ON THE COMB AS OUTWARD AND VISIBLE SIGN

Her white hair's been wind-ruffed—
   the way a dandelion's haloed globe

drifts open—& when my mother
   stops, four steps inside our home,

my father stops behind her, & draws
   her comb, blue as the Virgin's cloak,

from his pocket. With exquisite
   care he redeems each blown strand

into its proper curve, although she
   does not know she's mussed or

even that he combs, her arms already
   open to claim the hug she craves

from each of us—while the eager
   spaniel wreathes about our halted

bodies, while my husband waits
   to slip inside & shut the door

behind. It's as though every atom
   in the room lights here, on the comb,

on my father's office of attendance—
   he who abandoned what he thought

was a calling to the priesthood—
   leaving off the white collar,

shutting firmly behind him
   the brass-hinged seminary door

to step, bride glowing on his arm,
    into this other life of devotion,

vowing to make her life at last
    perfect, & she perfectly loved.

And here she stands, hair
    gleaming even while her mind

dims, as the ministering comb—
    blue as sky or Heaven—is raised

& stroked & lowered, & our family
    stops, lowering its head, to bow

again before the contract, the blessing.

PLEASED TO MAKE YOUR ACQUAINTANCE

I tell them again
the story of how they met.
On a bus, I say, after going
to the symphony. It was
an all-Beethoven program
on a Saturday night.
Dad, you asked if you could sit by her
on the ride back, and she
said yes. Later, a mutual friend
had you both for dinner.
You took it from there.

They smile at each other, pleased
with themselves and the good
fortune of those events, already
growing hazy in their minds.
In ten minutes time, they will
forget everything I've said, but
for now, they know each other's
face, voice, name.

They hold hands, a little shyly
ask me again
How did we meet?

AT THE ALZHEIMER'S CENTER

He's just dropped her off,
his wife of thirty-seven years.
For him, this is what mornings are now:
this gray mid-winter heaviness of sky,
this thing he must keep doing.
Their conversations are oddly casual
but with a strange circularity:
"Here we are, Martha," he'll say flatly;
"Oh? What is it?" she'll ask.
Sometimes he answers with a quiet smile,
but even when grief lurches through him
he's always tender.
"The Center, honey. It's time to go to the Center."
If you saw him later, in the aisles at Wal-Mart
or watching TV in his reclining chair,
you wouldn't know:
just an old blue-collar guy like a million others,
ball cap, graying mustache, bit of a swag-belly.
Old wolf in the lean deeps of winter,
he fights an inextinguishable hunger
hour after snow-muffled solitary hour—
fights even now as he pulls up to the hardware store,
not to glimpse in memory
the woman she was.

REMEMBERING

I visit every day at lunch time,
  bringing with me your favorite things:
        Biscuits from Loveless Cafe
        Chicken and dumplings from Cracker Barrel
        or those coconut covered marshmallows from Walmart.

Surrounded by those things you love:
        Our wedding day picture in that silver frame your
          Aunt Mable gave you on our 25th anniversary.
        A picture of David when you first tried to swaddle him.
        The quilt you made from all of your old dresses and my shirts.
        The hairbrush your mama gave you on your 18th birthday.

I brush your hair and sing some of the songs we love:
        Ring of Fire.
        Amazing Grace.
        Evergreen.
I wait for you to tell me to shut up, that I can't sing.
I look for a toe tap or your mouth to move at the chorus.
Nothing.

I watch you eat
  waiting for an expression of remembrance.
Nothing.
No hint that you have any special affection
  for the food or me.

Now I see you on Thursdays.
You rock by the window in that old wooden chair,
  the same one you rocked our baby boy in.
If he had lived past his twenty-second birthday
  he would have been sixty today.
You eat bland vegetables and cut up boiled chicken.
Your arms are moving fork to mouth—just muscle
  memory programmed to eat, with no feeling or expression.

Your eyes avoid my eyes like our puppy did
  when you caught him shredding up the
  morning newspaper.

They're still as blue as the ocean
    with little specks of silver.

You've left me and yet you are still here.
Your body is warm, your heart beating. I want
    to snuggle up against you and just sleep—it would
    seem adulterous since you have vacated your body.
You slipped away so gradually that I was not prepared.
When do I pack up your things and let you go?

Pastor Knight asked me on March 25th, 1956 if I
    would keep you in sickness and in health,
    for better or for worse.

I call on Sundays now and Nurse Karen
    puts the phone by your ear so I can tell
    you I love you.
I don't drive anymore—my eyes don't allow it.
The church brings me a plate lunch each day.
I eat at noon so we can eat together in spirit.

I've got all my favorite things around me:
            The baseball glove I gave David when he was six.
            The handkerchief you put in my pocket every
                morning when I was leaving for work that
                smelled of your perfume.
            The picture of the three of us on David's
                graduation day.

I eat the food the church brings, it doesn't
    taste like your cooking.
The old record is playing and I listen to
    Johnny and June.
I sing along and tell myself
            "I still can't sing."

But you already knew that.

DESTINATION UNKNOWN

Each day he packs. Takes pictures off the walls,
adds the dish that held his morning toast. The crumbs too.
One slipper goes into his bag. One stays under the bed.

He puts on a shirt, and another on top of it. And another.
Not interested in toothbrush, shaving cream, socks.
In his boxers and shirts, he packs. Destination unknown.

He once ruled a kingly intellect, his brain a mastermind
of the legal, the linear, the logical. Now it works a new
dimension, a marvel unto itself. Coordinates unknown.

Each night she dreams. Vows renewed, church bells
sounding. She sees the wedding dress, hears the music.
There is dancing and a cake with a bride on top, but no groom.

She keeps a ledger of all the losses, journals the little injuries
and all the goodbyes. Her reasons are complicated even
to herself. She thinks she hears a kind of poetry in it.

She says in wonder, *Now he likes to dance. He plays games
with his food. All day he rides the elevator up and down.*

Ready for lift off, he says. Destination unknown.

LIKE IT WAS

I want to be part of your program, he said.
There is no program.

I don't like it here. I want it like it was.
We all want it like it was.

Then where's the map?
There is no map.

But, listen, I love you.
And I love you.

Doesn't seem like it. Then why am I here?
You attacked me. You hurt me.

But I want to be on your program, he said.
There is no more program . . . .

ALZHEIMER'S RELAY

After fifty years, how can I not sink into that hollow
you made? Your hand curved along my shoulder.
The way morning light spilled over the ridge
of our hips blurring us, our arms more wave than
flesh. You turned, I turned, the strokes we made:
the same, the same.

                  No matter how far you
swim now, I will kick and will not lose you.

PICKING A BOUQUET OF RUSSIAN OLIVE

Their spicy-sweet fragrance reaches me
before I'm at the empty lot. Two weeks
early. They usually bloom in May.

I snap branches off these invasive trees,
being careful of thorns. Our home
will smell like Polynesia.

Walking back, I notice a pair of ladybugs
mating on one of the centimeter-or-so-
sized leaves. The one on top has ten spots
and is redder than the one underneath—
more orange, mostly hidden.

At our drive, my husband rests
on a garden bench—he's forgotten
to mow the lawn. This morning
he went outside to "go home"—pjs, shoes,
a National Geographic underarm.

I said he should shower, breakfast was ready.
"Where's the shower?" he asked,
and I showed him, told him he *was* home.

Last night, despite his twitchings
and bad dreams, he reached for me—
remembered love.

I'M MARRIED TO YOU

Even when you forget who I am,
you make me feel loved.
At breakfast you ask courteously
as of a stranger,
Are you married?

I'm married to you.

Oh! you say and,
straightening your spine,
tilt your head in a preening motion.
Your satisfied smile
comforts me all day.

Patricia Lapidus

TOGETHER

Your mind
began to drop
pieces
into the river
like bones sifting down.
You forgot
the children's names.
You forgot
how to cook an egg.
You forgot
you didn't love me.
You forgot
you ever said
you didn't love me.
I tried to tell you
our sad story,
but it was trying to
unpeace
your mind from the river where
bones and stories dissolve.
My sieving fingers lifted
empty from the water. You said,
"I'm glad we are together."
I accepted your last truth
as your best truth.
A shiny new story.
Together
we smiled.

ROOMS WITHOUT SHADOWS

Perhaps the textures (layers of carpets, dark wood,
dull silver, velvet pillows, faded photographs, books,
paintings, unwashed glasses)
deflect the effects of light in the same way they mute sounds.
I see you move against the lamp,
but only the faintest softening of color on the bare bits of wall
and nothing on the floor precedes you, nor do you make a sound.

Confirming that I live alone, though you are here,
sleepy, hungry, whiskey-drinking ghost who is disappearing
day by day. Handsome still; quiet, serene, increasingly transparent,
shrouded in latent grandeur and charm. Generous; forgetting beneficiaries.
Forgetting, too, the simplest forms of love—no sign, no word left.
It seems you do not mind at all who you are now.
I, however, mind terribly who you no longer are.

Perhaps in the drawers you leave ajar your shadow, like a robe, folds itself
neater than we. Tapes accumulate dust, too clotted to play. We live
surrounded by ever more and softer things and they,
as they age with us, darken, blur, disintegrate,
absorbing our energies, erasing the effects of our passing,
bleaching out our shades and stilling all our songs.

Leslie Gerber

EROSION

You told me once
soaking the porcelain lining
of your antique bathtub
would damage it.
After every bath,
you would wipe it carefully
with your towel,
a task now left
to me, the one who
remembers things.
Strange
to think that water hurts
something made to contain it—
the way I, meant to contain
your love, am now eroding.

ESSENTIAL ACT

I swim at two levels:
on the surface with my usual
world of words, phone calls,
the daily venturing forth
to fulfill tasks in a public forum
ignorant of your decline,
and at a submerged level
where, holding my breath,
I float you one more day
into a shrinking future.

When tired I ask myself,
which is worse, fear that he will die
or fear that his memory
will turn the corner and forget me.

The answer might surprise
those who think
staying alive
the one essential act.

GOING HOME

> I lift up my eyes to the hills.
> From where does my help come?
> —Psalm 121

Today, we read a Psalm together.
The Heavenly Father offers us long-term protection
and my scientist-husband says,
That's comforting.

He also says, *It's not religious,*
curious why no mention of Jesus or salvation.

All these years he's never referred to Jesus
except when I scrape through an intersection
on a yellow light or when the hammer deflects
and mashes his thumb.

Who knew he'd be comforted by the beauty of words
called up over millennia? by looking to the Bible
even as he hears the resolute thump of death's march?

Now he tells me, *I want to go home.*
I tell him he is home. Here on this couch
in this living room. *This is your home—here with me.*
A nod of the head, a grudging agreement,
but that's not the home he longs for.

The Color of Her Eyes

These lilacs, he says, are the color of her eyes
the day we wed, the color of her eyes the day
she died. They grew from a shoot she cut from
a root in the yard of the house she left when she
wished to marry me. Her mother wished I was
Catholic. I wished to do the right thing. We married
in May when I promised her mother—the priest—to
raise Catholics. The yard of the house we bought
was dirt. We seeded grass, planted lilac, raised
that child, then two and more until there were five
and none of them were Catholic. These lilacs grew
in the yard of this house we kept for fifty years. In
April she died. The lilacs were late but her eyes
bloomed. I sat beside her bed that wasn't ours.
She opened her eyes and I smiled. She held my
hand. In the end and the beginning your hands hold.
In between you waste all your chances to let go.
She looked at me. We must have remembered
something like love, and then she closed her eyes
and I was gone.

The house is yours now and the yard.

WALK ON WATER

THIS BODY

I cannot get out of this body.

This body cannot get
out of its role as caregiver.

As caregiver I am not allowed
to go anywhere or do anything
that takes me away from taking care.

Taking care of her is demanding.
It means I must always make certain
that she has enough to eat
and that she does eat it.

Eat it carefully. Chew and swallow
with more attention
than she devotes to most things.
Most things have lost their interest
for her. She likes to sit and be quiet.

Be quiet, friend, when this body demands
a kind of companionship
it will never experience again.
You may live to be one hundred
but you know she will outlive you
and that you will never be free.

Be free to enjoy the attentions
of the other women clustered around you,
admiring the care and devotion you give her,
wishing they had the same from some man,
even me, while they are still able to appreciate him.
It might indeed be me, except that
I cannot get out of this body.

DOWN AND AROUND

I have been the Chinese proverb
If two men feed a horse it will stay thin
I have been law abiding
and the laws I have abided by
from time to time I have broken
like the hard thoughts I have broken

across my forehead
from Eastern Daylight to Pacific Daylight
been sober with my mother
when we've lugged my father
carried his anger, his body
his Alzheimer's mind to a bathroom.

I have been the horse
I have been the hay and I have been
sickled, baled, unbaled
chewed up for fuel
slid down and around
a thousand-pound stomach
excreted into handsome green balls
fertilizing rose beds.

I have been the fertilizer
I have been the rose
so how about it, Sugar Lips?
In the spongy autumn twilight
let's march inside this bar
and take whatever blessings
the beer gives us.

My Cheating Heart

Sometimes, if she's not all that very wet,
    and not a bit dirty down there when I peek,
        I check my mother out of her nursing home
without changing a thing—even if it means
    that I will have to spray the car with Lysol later
        and spray extra Lysol on her wheelchair
before we go into the coffee shop for coffee
    and her favorite cinnamon bun warmed over
        in the microwave for the two of us to share.
My mother likes to open the door to Java J's herself,
    wheeling through the tables and chairs she calls beautiful
        and past the mural of Venice painted on the wall.
Once we got to the cash register to order and a little girl stared,
    the glasses on her face reminding me of my mother's glasses
        that she wore from four to eighty-four and doesn't now.
It wasn't the wheelchair that caught her eye but my mother's kitten,
    her favorite stuffed toy that she traded for a moment with the girl,
        who handed her a small plastic purple horse with
            sparkling hair
that made my mother's eyes light up and made me forget she was wet,
    as wet as a toddler but not quite as wet as an 85-year-old can get
        after drinking watered-down coffee off and on since dawn.
The coffee shop we go to always smells like coffee beans,
    the rich aroma of my mother's favorite drink masking all else,
        the hot coffee as intoxicating as the cold wine she
            used to drink.

AT THE MIDNIGHT DINER

—after Nikky Finney

The two of us, seated in our booth, a Formica sea
stretched dumb between us. And you thumb the pillar of sugar,
its hinged tab of open and shut a puzzle to you now, more profound
perhaps than ponderings on time or god. You take a stab instead
at shreds of lettuce, slipping, one by one, like sloughed syllables
falling senselessly to your plate. The stainless steel tines
of memory, one might observe, are useless as that fork
in your hand; the one you try, bleary-headed, to comb through your hair,
the one that defies your crumple-knuckled fingers now. No use
looking back to days when you could chopstick a mound of rice,
hula-hoop ringed onions on your fork, skate-swirl linguine tresses
against the hungry belly of your spoon—and then when sated
flip credit card from pouch in purse, calculate a tip, dance
the letters of your name across the line—no. Now
neurons clatter dully like ice cubes against the plastic
chamber of the cup that jitters against your lip. Mama,
I don't remember you
feeding me. Too long ago,
I guess, but I'll remember this:
lifting sliced tomato to your mouth, yes. Mama,
chew, swallow, chew once more. Our pas de deux
of mother-daughter, daughter-mother—no more
heartbreaking than this bowl scraped clean,
or that paper napkin, forgotten on the floor,
or the discarded paper sheath, shed there
from your lipstick-kissed plastic straw.

LEANING

"It's only June," he said.
"How can the maple leaves
already lean towards orange?"
I should have told him then
that I liked his word, "lean,"
as if the trees, weary from early
summer heat, looked for a shadow
to rest against. My father sat
breathless on a park bench,
ten steps from the car too much
for his lungs, the glare of the sun
too much for his tired mind. Across the lot
children dove into the crowded pool,
their parents shouting warnings
from the lounge chairs where they rested
in the shade, telling stories
of old summers to each other.
I handed my father triangle halves
of a peanut butter sandwich. His favorite.
Our lives were sometimes difficult.
He had done the best he could.
I watched his jaw move deliberately as he
chewed and swallowed, chewed and swallowed.
There was nothing then I wouldn't have done for him.

Therese Halscheid

My Father's Cereal

We wake on dry land where the sun works brilliant—

until a bib is tied about my father's neck
a bowl is placed high upon books

and the largest spoon in the house is set in his hand
between two crooked fingers.

There is my mother creating this daily scene of events
pouring Cheerios into his bowl

adding the white milk before guiding
my father's spoon down into it.

She leaves the room then, and there is only myself
sitting across from him.

I have my own bowl but do nothing about it.

We are a pair, of sorts. I refuse how his face is unreadable
that his brain is damaged enough to believe he is eating

and he is blind to the point where he thinks I look fine.

When we move, we move as slow water moves
barely along, because nothing can save us.

His spoon floats through air, is empty, is treading in space.
My thoughts are all garbled as if made of liquid . . . .

We remain this way, my father and I
as if under water.

The Cheerios turn soggy, inflating like inner tubes
but it is too late—

soon we will drown in this moment

day will begin, and there will only be the strange surfacing
of our tragic lives.

THE SHAVE

Holding out my left hand
I dispense a small
billowing cloud into its center.

Tilting my father's head
a little, dipping into the
pure white puff, I begin to work
it into his coarse gray stubble.

After some careful deliberation
on the starting point, I pull the razor
across his slack cheek—but without
tension the blade
            stutters and skips.

  This will not work!

So I ask him—show him how—
to make a face.

  See like this.

My chin jutting forward and up
      like the bow of a ship.
      He copies my form and the razor glides
      through the white foam.

Next we steer the ship left and then right
      moving across an ocean of loss, until we are done.

My father touches his cheek and smiles
at the renewed smoothness of his face
and I realize that sometimes memory is less about
the act and more about trust.

What someone knows
when they know nothing else.

Felicia Mitchell

Notes on the Lost Art of Seduction

He sees a woman he wants to touch.
I see somebody else whose flesh
is as impenetrable as a hymen.
At the threshold of desire,
I find myself hesitant to enter,
the reflection of my mother's body
glancing off my younger body,
a chaperone or bucket of cold water.
How do I get from here to there,
from the mole on her stomach
to the mole just like it on my breast?
From the labia she washes in front of me
to my own private netherworld?
How can he touch my shoulders
without touching hers?
When my mother and I shower,
her naked and me fully clothed,
there are no boundaries between us.
Where my skin ends, her skin begins,
and I croon so she feels safe with me,
as safe as I would like to feel with him.
But I'm as slippery as my mother
is with me when she smells of lavender.
I am a bar of soap or naïve girl,
as likely to slip out of his hands
as my mother is to slip out of mine
if I don't hold on to her holding on to me.
I forget who needs protection
when I leave that bathroom
where steam replaces a lover's breath.
When I close my eyes,
and try to let him touch my skin,
I see my mother's one breast, a signpost
pointing to a place I am afraid to go.

PERFECT FORGIVENESS

He left his wife and threw his back out
packing books and clothes into his Toyota
and drove in hybrid pain to his Aunt Edie's
who lived with her dementia in a house in Easton

and stayed with her for a time and every day
she was pleasantly surprised to see him
and asked him what he did to his back
and asked him what he did to his marriage

and the repetition was good for him and good
for her because she couldn't remember and he
was beginning to forget just why he'd left
as the days passed and his loneliness increased

so they sat together at her kitchen table
and he told the painful story again and again
and each time he told it a little differently
and each time she heard it for the first time

and shook her head at the same sad and truly
unforgivable parts which were all true
and took his plate to the sink and promptly forgot
took his plate and washed it completely clean

LOOKING AT BOOBS WITH AUNT EDIE

Me and my Aunt Edie are looking
at my parents' wedding album.
My parents are dead; my Aunt Edie
is living with dementia; I'm fifty
and twice divorced—just to give you
an idea, a preamble. On the first page:
a photo of my mother and grandmother.
Aunt Edie's short-term memory is shot,
but she can still remember the name
of her fourth grade teacher, her best friend
from camp, her great Aunt Millie, Uncle
Donald, and the exact number of the house
on Observantenvech where she lived
in Maastricht until she was eight: #46. "Hey,
look how busty Saftah looks," she says,
and we stare awhile at my grandmother's
boobs. I smile, nod, turn the page
to a photo of my mother and grandfather
walking down the aisle arm-in-arm. "Hey,
look how pointy Reggie's boobs are here,"
says Aunt Edie. And I can't help noticing
the theme that's developing page by page,
breast by breast. And I'm wondering if
this is a side of Aunt Edie that was always
there, only covered up, inhibited, corseted
like her own ample breasts ("which were
always much bigger than your mother's,"
she tells me now) and only coming out
in her late seventies because she's forgotten
the reason for keeping it hid. Whatever
the reason, her celebration of the bosoms
of the women of my family is making me
squirm. That's when she looks up, adjusts
her bra strap, fixes me with a penetrating
hazel arrow, and says, "If I didn't know you
better, nephew, I'd say you were blushing."

THE WALK HOME

Each day the curtains part from each home we pass
and without clearly seeing them
I can sense the widening eyes of mothers, I can feel
their thoughts through the windows
and it is all about the way
my father and I look
to them.

It is about it being late spring and the fact that
he and I wear woolen coats and gloves
as we are always cold, our lives so dark
not even the sun can
save us.

It is about my looking less than human, brittle-boned
slumped, I am that thin—

and certainly, it is the sight of my father beside me
who is near blind and brain damaged
someone behaving in ways that one might find
in mental wards.

Sometimes, their curtains are torn far apart
so fast as if fate landed an illusion, something
that never should be, and nothing appears real
except for their manicured lawns
and the distance the sidewalks allow
each afternoon at 3:00, as we shuffle past this
place of groomed grass and the scent of
immediate flowers.

Above us are always the
overhanging trees whose blossoming
leaves spread glorious and are just like
a wedding arbor.

So perfect, I think, for this really is
what we are married to—

this aisle, this arm-in-arm walk
after school from my aunt's house to ours
this street like an obvious map of us
pointing things out that
we cannot escape.

THE SCARF

I didn't want a scarf. I didn't
need a scarf. I just wanted her busy.
There in assisted living—barely
assisted and not really living—
her mind slowly peeling off with
nothing but Bingo and television.
Staring out the window.
                              A project,
a project. Heavy hours require
a project. I talked her into a scarf.
Even with trembling hands and
a ruffled retina she could handle
a task that simple, for wasn't she
queen of yarn and the cable stitch?
Master of wool and bouclé and
oh, that royal blue dress, knit
when she was still Pierce-Arrow
sleek and beautiful?
                              She chose
purple, had the clerk in the store
cast the stitches. Ninety-one years
she trod upon this earth. My job
for the next five, the final five,
was working to keep her out of it.
Two bouts of pneumonia, broken
bones, a crashed wheelchair,
and the crowning blow, dementia.
Meanwhile, I played cheerleader
for a scarf, overjoyed with over-
seeing how it grew: gluttonous
as a boa constrictor fed on the
purple it was made of. A royal
lengthening to lengthen the little
time she had left.

Now, whenever
I wear it, I have to wrap it twice
around my throat, then fling the ends
back over both shoulders, wrestling
it into a double knot. A thirty-footer
with twelve inches of fringe, con-
ceived as a hoax to prove that what
one loves can live forever the way
it was. Like Penelope at her loom,
she kept those needles going so I
could keep *her* going. Trouble was,
there were no suitors to distract her
and no hero-hope of rescue. No one
but me, inheritor of this squeeze,
this choke hold wound around my neck.

ABSENCE

Stay put I tell my dad, like a parent warning an impulsive child to behave in her absence. I leave the car running, heat blowing, knowing he can't follow me on his blown out knee even if he forgets why I left him or who I am or when I'll return and I will not let him freeze in my absence. Coatless

into the wind I cross the lot, halogen lit, past freezing cars, parked without passengers, fingers stinging and clutching his prescription for pain. Inside, I follow

signs and more signs through a maze of make-up, of medicine, to the rear where I wait and keep waiting, while behind the counter

the pharmacist under bright lights is rushing, and then I am too, back toward the exit—but here he comes, limping through the electric door waving my coat sleeves open like a father tracking a forgetful child— like a father who won't let me freeze.

TO EARTH SOFTLY SETTLES

She runs, away, like a wind
that shakes the shutters
   I've got to go   rattles
the heart of her daughter
who folds her white cane
and cries and tries,
and cries again, *Wait! Mom! Wait!*

Mom runs like a wind
unmoored,
unleashed on an ocean of sails—
her outstretched arms
those broken booms, the jibs
of fear, free and falling
a wind like a breath to earth softly settles
the wordless tempest withering within.

I couldn't stop, she tells her daughter
like apology, like admission,
like loss, but more
like disaster.

ICON

when you tumble   in the shower
I rush right over   & praise Whomever

no bones broken   only shaken   & you
shrunken   in your blue   bathrobe

aides & nurses   wandering off
to never-ending   dismal   duties

neighbors too   to rehearse   routine
unlovely   idiosyncrasies

slumped on the couch   you   lean against me
then slowly   unfold   the crumpled

parchment of your body   to lie across my lap
if anyone   returns   they'll see

living sculpture   almost familiar
son & mother   perverse Pietà

REVELATION

Startled by his bare foot
hidden all these years
beneath black socks, I look
at my father's bone whiteness
standing on a dark braided rug,
see his slender toes, their fragile
grip on his world, and a large
angular bunion, a secret burden
he's pressed beneath him
for much of eighty-five years.

He has asked me to help him—
something he's never asked before—
to clip his split nail that keeps snagging,
like memory, on tiny threads.

I am motionless,
lost in the whiteness of this foot.

TRAINING NEW AIDES: ONE THING I'M TIRED OF

Trying to make it look easy, so no huffing and puffing, not even breathing, just talking and lifting, nice and smooth, maybe even gesturing with one hand, maybe even gesturing with both hands, maybe even closing my eyes. Like "I could do this blindfolded with my hands behind my back." Like "I could do this and take care of a two-year-old and make breakfast at the same time." Like, "This isn't impossible. This isn't ridiculous." What are we trying to sell?

What are we trying to buy?

SELF TALK

Girl, what's with these
long yawns and heavy sighs?
Step back and take the long view.

Eventually each one
becomes a burden
to those who love them.

Give it ten years and your life, too,
will shrink to a bed and tray table.
Someone—paid or volunteer—

will have to comfort you
when your mind wanders
the long corridors of night.

SALVAGE

THE POEM GERONIMO

Is written at seventy miles per hour with second driver
up front and he (yes, that's really his name, Geronimo)
black hair combed smoothly back from his brow
(think: crow's wing in the wind here) bends over
my mother in the ambulance to change her diaper, returning
her home from the hospitals of the north to die in the desert,
her own bit of heaven: couch by the TV, bed by the white-
curtained window, rabbits under the yellow lounge chairs,
a glimpse of the orange tree, laden, through the patio window.

She can see me reading in the living room under the yellow
rain of the lamp in my favorite chair;
I can see her reading in her bed by the yellow
rain of the lamplight...

The poem Geronimo is written at seventy miles per hour and he
answers (think: the essence of upright kindness here) "I've got
babies, I'm used to diapers!" to her questioning look,
speeding past almond orchards in full bloom...
Is this really happening to me, and this young man
with the movie star face is changing my diaper?

At seventy miles per hour without losing balance, without bumping
his head on the overhanging glass full of life-saving equipment.
At seventy, without losing humane dignity, rolling the 93-year-old
patient back and forth as the job demands and then, 10 minutes later,
as the infected bladder squirts, returning with a joke and a smile to do
it again (think: angel here, a term I do not use lightly) asking me
meanwhile if I'm OK as we speed past the hawk poised on its
fence post listening, listening in the crosswinds of the cars to
swoop down on the little rustling being under the grass and take her
while the light of love shines out of the eyes of all of us...

Geronimo.

CHANGING SEASON

Seven days since I delivered you
to the nursing home—our home
left forever, and you, in your dementia,
more fortunate than I in not knowing.
A house empty of you, my love.
Now I must drive to where you are.

When not visiting you, I erase traces,
reminders of the almost
unbearable years I cared for you,
when I gave myself in the hope
you might get well. Leaves fall,
vees of geese airborne to an elsewhere.

Gone, boxes of Depends, rubber gloves,
disinfectant wipes, cans of Lysol—
your walker, wheelchair. In one week's time
you went downhill—unable to walk,
falling every day—the need to call neighbors,
workmen repairing the chimney, the police.

I put back hall rugs, unlock windows,
unbolt doors, bring out scissors
and nail clippers from hiding places—
remove plastic pads from our bed,
return the spread and pillow shams,
the doll you once bought me.

It's quiet, quiet as the garden without
the summer songbirds.
Lulled by all the years we were given,
somehow I didn't prepare for the season.

CLEANING HOUSE

Mom, you've gone to the facility.
I can put things back
in their intended spaces
without fear of you co-opting them
as personal playground toys.

Bar soap and deodorant
you sometimes used as toothpaste
are home inside the bathroom.

My purple toothbrush that would tempt you
need not by my bedside be.

The toilet paper's out of hiding.
Three sit on the upright holder
knowing they won't be transported
elsewhere.

The trash I redirected
when I caught you
sifting, sorting, and recycling
is rerouted to the right receptacle.

Your car keys have resurfaced—
"discovered" in the lies I told
about their disappearance.

My memories—bagged, emotions—canned
and stashed upon the highest kitchen shelf
when I became your cook, your driver,
private shopper, nurse, and janitor
are now in hand and open
ready for their placement
in my head and heart.

I finally emerge—free
to be the weeping daughter
I'm supposed to be.

THE PRETTY AIDE AT THE NURSING HOME,

you tell us, doesn't remember her own name,
forgets she used to work in another town

two hours away at Hiester Lanes
where, for thirty years, you bowled near-perfect games

in that other life where you walked and drove
and lived sometime long before now in this unfamiliar town

near us, where she insists she's always lived.
Daily, she smiles, shakes her head, claims she's never held

a bowling ball, cheered loudly for your league
or any other, never learned to keep score.

Still, after trimming your toenails,
rubbing lotion on your cracked skin,

adjusting the TV to *American Bowling Congress,*
and re-filling your empty paper cup, she's remembered

to sneak in an extra sugar cookie, leftover
from yesterday's Valentine's Day party

from which she wheeled you back to your room
early when you began to weep for what she refuses,

even now, to recall of a life she did not have,
in a town she's never seen,

at a place she did not work, using the name
that you insist she declines, even now, to remember.

LUNCH ON THE ALZHEIMER'S UNIT

Blank stares
Bathroom smells
And noises
Drooling
Food dribbling onto shirts
Yelling
Crying
Spilled milk
She tries to put the wrong end of the spoon in her mouth
Tries to drink from the salt shaker
Licks the plate
Banging, repeated banging
Repeated vocal syllables
Coughing
Gagging
Fingers full of pudding

And the gentle caregivers
All women (underpaid to be sure)
Carefully
Wipe and
Feed
Mop up and
Smile
Cajole and
Soothe
Wipe up again
And again and again and again and again
All the while
Taking bites
Of their own lunch

In the midst of this
Hell
They are grace
Embodied
Jesusettes
Come to save
Those of us
Who can't/won't
Live with this daily bread
They give us this day
And forgive us our trespasses
They deliver us
From evil

Hallowed be their names

Lucia
Lacramoira
Ebony
Julia
Fanny
Aleta

May theirs be the
Queendom
And the power
And the glory
Forever and ever

Amen

STEVE

The night before you died, I talked too much.
I asked about the show, the fan, the sprinklers
(on or off, Steve? does it bother you, Steve?)

I asked about your squeezy pouch of fruit,
your cup of chocolate pudding, your soup
(good or bad, Steve? are you sure you're done, Steve?)

I asked if I could hold your hand. I asked
if you were sad or scared or sleepy yet
(does your foot hurt, Steve? want your comb, Steve?)

I asked you all my questions, and I used
your name a hundred times, like yelling at
a dog to stay and not chase cars too far.

I thought you tried to slap me, like before,
but your wife said that lately, you had been trying
to hold people's faces in your hands.

Carol Tyx

THINGS MY MOTHER CAN'T FIND AFTER BREAKING HER PELVIS

Her apartment: the recipe for spinach quiche
on the kitchen counter, the spinach
in the freezer. Her nail file,
the orange pound cake she bought
at the bake sale, the floss threader
for her bridge, her checkbook
with Clara Catherine in the corner.

Her cane: if only she had her cane
she could hoist herself
out of this wheelchair and
onto the commode and
what do you mean she can't
have her cane until her pelvis heals?

E-pisss-co-pal-ian: the word her best friend
passed on to her before she died
that helps you pee when your aide is watching
and you can't get things started.

Her name: *Clara*, a young woman
with a West African accent calls out.
My mother stares at her smeared plate.
Clara's my grandmother, she tells her tablemates.
I'm Katie, have been for years.

How to call for help: push the button.
Where's the button? Around your neck.
What do I do with it? Push it.
I already pushed it.
Is the light on?
No. So what should you do?
Push the button. Yes.

IN AN ANGRY VEIN

Last night, I dreamed again—
adult potty chairs and corridors,
cottage cheese and peaches on a tray.
Nothing that shines. Not even language
to pull me out and awake. No metaphor
to wrap my new life in, only a jumble
of paraphernalia and the red button
she pushes and pushes for no one to come.

Yesterday I did her nails,
held each trembling finger to file
and swab, cream with Intensive Care.
The veins bulging across each ache
and knob, down each arthritic knuckle,
weaving a net to hold them. Poor veins.
Mama's veins. Tote bag for bones.
Each cord, bruise-blue and swollen
as a traffic jam or a telephone wire
clogged with voices desperate to get out.

We play a game of cassino. She naps, stirs,
asks again when dinner's served
and where. I push her in her chair,
earning my ticket (my sister says) to heaven.
My sister's wrong.

A little girl holds her breath
for ninety years. The veins labor,
wrestle with their knots. A story, a story.
Little girl needs to dredge up the story.
And I, for the life of me, don't have the heart
to make her ream it out.

Sandra Berris

ADJUSTMENT

Late afternoons Mother wanders
the corridors of the nursing home.
She looks for a way out
to a place where she
can recognize herself.

She's gone from her narrow kitchen
once brightened with pink Formica
where she stood for hours in front
of her old gas stove, satisfied
stirring stews or soups, roasting chickens.

Now she can't boil water, the simplest
of tasks. She spends her days wandering
through rooms of other patients,
filling a shopping bag with treasures—
someone's pair of cheap earrings, a borrowed
polyester dress two sizes too large, a terrycloth
robe with tears at the hem. The nurses and I
laugh when she tells us she's tired,
having spent the day *shopping*.

But late at night I can't laugh
when she grows restless again
and is walking the corridors. She
and the others pass each other
again and again trapped like fish
in this waterless bowl. Outside
are flowers and a bench in the garden
where she's not allowed to go.

Each night she re-hides her purse
in a new spot under her mattress,
packs earrings, a dress and a robe
in her pillowcase, ready for her escape.
I know she's standing by the phone
but can't remember anyone's number.

ALYSSUM

My mother calls from her nursing home.
She says, get me out of here. Her voice
is forceful. I say, what's wrong.
There were spiders lined up around
my bed last night, she says, they didn't
move. I held still until they went away.
I don't remember when or where they
had gone to. Not this, not this she says
to her undying self. There were white flies
in my garden and they hovered over
the sweet alyssum and when I went out
to see them they left me, the ground
cover left me, and the yard was barren,
the fruit trees were barren. And where
everything had gone I do not know.
I could touch nothing and nothing
could touch me. And there was no place,
there was no place. Perhaps the gods
she says, are jealous of death. They hold
you until you are still and then they leave
you because they do not care. Faith
does not prove anything. Why
won't you, she says? I say, I can't, let's talk
about this tomorrow. She hangs up on me.
Ten minutes later she calls again.
She asks, are you all right. You're doing
too much, leave the laundry go. I say
I'll see you tomorrow. She says, good,
get some rest.

Kelly DuMar

WHO DOES NOT LOVE A WALL

In the unit called Memory Care he grows
wild and young as a colt restless to sow his
oats and goddammit he will find the exit or
die trying, there's a wilderness out there
stretches for miles—he's got his eyes right
on it—but some jackass actually built this
wall this way so he can see out but not get
out and some son of a bitch stole all those
things you sit on out here so there's nothing
to stack and climb to scale the wall and before
I built a wall like this, he says like somebody
who said it first, I'd ask to know what I was
walling in or walling out and to whom I was
like to give offense and what he knows but
doesn't say is if there's a wall and a will

Andrena Zawinski

THE WAY IT IS

She staunchly insists her single hospital bed
in the shared room with drawn blue curtain
is a wing of her private and sprawling apartment,
kindly offers to have lunch staff heat something up
at what she introduces as the spa she now owns.
She won't allow the television or music
that distract from her invisible manuscript.

She sits in dimming light in an eclipsing eve,
wanes small and thin. This is what it has become.

She vows, in yet another delusional bloom,
to incorporate tai chi into her yoga practice
while she is able only to stand then wobble
and drop into the wheelchair she is too weak
to roll. She demands her lipstick, the stolen clothes
she squirreled away under the table, ferreting
the latest escape route, then the passport

she needs to fly off in this phantasmagoria,
longing a gnawing hunger. This is the way it goes.

Under night's fading clouds, meteors shower
across stroked occipital and parietal lobes.
She wades through a trough of fog, confused
by the distance between herself and the world.
Jupiter kisses Juno. Venus births Cupid. Mars
is at odds with everyone, noisy, keeping her up
under the same sky that holds the rest of us

silent and still, eyes aflutter with spirits of dream
as we drift off into sleep. This is the way it is.

Richard M. Berlin

NURSING HOME DOCTORS

After each lap around the circular hall
the aides smile, "Hello, Doctor!"
and he nods at their greetings
like a general inspecting his troops.
Dressed in the frayed polyester suit
I saw him wear on hospital rounds,
he cradles a baby blue chart, and stops
at random doorways to review his records.
I say "good morning" and he studies me
in my white coat, like a skin lesion
he has seen only once in a textbook.
And I lead him to the door with a shingle
posted outside, his old oak desk
laid out with a blotter, fountain pen,
and a spoon for applesauce he eats
while he writes long, illegible reports,
falling asleep hours past midnight,
just as he did during forty years of practice,
in the arms of his worn out leather chair.

NURSING HOME BLUES

"Hi Handsome," I say and he says "Hi Babe."
He's subdued in his wheelchair
playacting who he used to be:
"I'm having a great time—but where's the bar?"
I still love him ferociously
but I put him here, I did it
like one of those guys who murders his wife
and then tells you how much he misses her.
The nutritionist says he doesn't eat his dinner.
The physical therapist says he says, "Go Away."
The nurse says he says, "You're fired."

But love doesn't recognize
demerits.

Leslie Gerber

What We Want

What I want
is for her to rise and walk
to say my name,
to say her name.
What she wants
is another spoonful of fruit.

What I want
is to sit by the fire
on a cold Cape Cod night,
wind yelling outside,
and talk about the movie we just saw,
how the kids are doing,
what's in today's paper.

What she wants
is to get her face away from my kiss,
although she might want the next one.

I want
to take her away from this place
where smiling women in purple shirts
are patiently teaching her
to walk again.

She wants them
to leave her alone.

I do not know
what I want anymore.
So much is gone
that I don't know what
to miss first.

She misses things too,
but not knowing what they are
seems to make it easier.

ALONE

Late at night, lying in bed
with no company except
my dog and my hand,
I embrace this moment
as a figure of speech
for my present.

My wife lies in
an electric bed
a few miles away,
pissing into a tube
and saying no
to almost everything.

The manuals I've read
on how to live
somehow omitted this chapter.

When hope is on vacation
you have to rely on
your own diminished resources.
Fun is a strange idea.
Joy lives on the moon.

But the hand that feels
so damn sorry for itself
is still moving this pen.

WHAT PASSES THROUGH THIS WORLD CRIES

Midnight. I walk beyond the reach
of lights into rough-mown pasture, soak
my shoes in the day's late shower. A full moon
gleams through clouds like high-beams
through fog, silhouettes two geese that soar
overhead, one silent but for its wingbeats,
the other squawking its distress.

At the nursing home where I've spent
three panicked days, my mother's learning
to sleep until wakened by strangers
who come to change her sodden diaper,
careful with the purple wound, black stitches
of her broken left hip. They tell me she clings
to the bed rail, wails my name.

In daylight, she watches every car
that enters the parking lot, looks a question
at me with each strange new sound: the blast
of air when the door opens, intended to keep out
flies, the beep-beep of a truck backing up.

It's the questions I can't answer—
how the brain smooths to calm unrippled
water, tiny flickers
of thought, how the body outlives
its memory of putting fork
to mouth, of thirst,
how a woman
becomes a silhouette of herself—

Questions that send me out, disturbed
as geese frightened from a pond
where they'd hoped to drift
through the warm humid night,
lush with the scent of wild roses,
a whippoorwill that won't stop
its plaintive song.

SALT

THE GOOD NEWS

upon receipt of an untimely sympathy card

The good news is that you are wrong.
He's still alive, he's here with us.
No hungry death has taken him.

His children don't wear black
or weep in waves
both night and day.

He's still alive, he's here with us.
Yet each day less
the one he was.

Some days
it seems
a stranger's come
to sit down in his chair,
an unkempt stranger
who squirrels away
the past in trinkets
and the present in

small bits of paper
stashed beneath his bed,
as if to build a nest there.

On good days
he folds the laundry,
shirt after shirt, matching socks.

Bad days,
a single
thick
blue
towel
sits on the heap
of socks and sheets.

A thick blue towel
splayed about.

The good news is that you are wrong.
The bad news is that you are right.

Nursing Home

when oaks molt they
broadcast leaves twice

as far as the tree is tall almost
like cottonwood

which descends seeds a quarter mile on
the wind as spit does

you must rake forever to clean up
elms

suffering from that dutch disease
just shed she

cant contain herself

shame

elms provide much shade from
april to october

you need to keep those bags near
december comes too soon

all that time

the sum of a man stuffed in a sack

MY MOTHER POUNDS THE DOOR OF PARADISE

My mother pounds the door
of Paradise. They won't
let her in. God
is a drummer.
Business has been
brisk lately.

Lord, she's thin!
Her mother's father
called her Quiet Dove
who's raised this clatter now.
While You've waxed great,
O God Grown Corpulent
on Fatter Fare,
she's pecked
where sparrows
strew the floor.
You don't deal
in doves
or sparrows
anymore.

Her hands are clean,
dipped three times
in the moon-drowned
river's cup. She stumbled
at the shore—but crossed.
Let her approach
your loftiness, Lord.
Speak! At you
I shake her skull
that rattles
with the die
you cast inside
but won't take up.

ANOTHER KIND OF TRUTH

Aunt Suzanne died in the early morning, the last stage of Alzheimer's ending with a sigh. Her grey matter resting now, after the kaleidoscopic firing of random neurons, memories, the confused details of a life blurring indiscriminately—where a banana is indeed a hammer or a husband, and death another kind of living.

REFLECTION

As I care for my mother,
deep in her dementia,
I too begin
to drop my nouns,
misplace them,
substitute vowels,
begin words
with the wrong consonant,
say *worry up* instead of *hurry up*—

her dementia, perhaps,
nibbling at me too
like a moth on lace.

What if the same dark confusion
takes root in my brain.

Today you and I
leave her behind,
as always confined
to her comfy bed,

drive to the cemetery
where she'll share a plot
with her husband
who got there first.

We say kaddish, holding hands,
the granite memorial shines,
the words *Together for Eternity*
sharply carved, greedy, expectant.

I see myself reflected
in the stone.

Saving against Alzheimer's

How do you save your nouns and your verbs?
Do you write them in a notebook and keep it with you?
Do you tie them in brightly colored silk scarves?

A blue scarf for water, as it flows upon the rocks,
under the bridge, fills the river, sings of love
and sorrow. Knot it about your neck. Do not forget.

Take your red scarf, the color of blood, the color of life.
Into it put memories of your babies, your husband,
the war he didn't survive. Knot it, twice. Do not lose.

Your white scarf holds your prayers and tears, the
mourning of what might have been but can never be.
Gather your sadness, remember it, respect it. Tie the knot tight.

Fill your yellow scarf with happiness. The bliss
of laughing babies, your first published poem,
happy times with good friends, the joys of discovery.

Knot that scarf over your heart; hold it tight. Keep the
good nouns close, the happy verbs a part of your life. Hold
onto the scarves, the knots, as you sail off the bridge.

Your nouns and your verbs will survive.

Richard M. Berlin

Cutting Toenails

After I slipped
my finger inside and felt
death's rough stone
I knew I should grant
the demented man's wish:
Just cut my toenails.
Down on my knees
I admired them, thick
as a silver dollar,
long and curved as
the *shofar*, the ram's horn
Jews blow on judgment day.
And I was dressed in white
like *Yeshua*, Jesus, my favorite
Jew, a healer I knew
would have been down
on his knees with me,
worshiping the beauty
of an old man's body.

I filled a vessel
with warm water,
soaked the nails soft,
washed the cracked
and calloused flesh,
and with my surgical steel
scissors cut sharp brown
crescents, like slivers
of a harvest moon,
imagining Yeshua,
what he atoned for
on Yom Kippur,
what pain he felt
for people he had not healed,
the expression in his eyes
when he heard the *shofar's* song
flying toward heaven.

Now I Lay Her Down

Awake, watching my mother rest, her shape
compacted in a troubled heap that heaves
and sighs, I think of what she was, as in
the Schubert lied her father sang, "Du bist
die Ruh"—You are rest.

            She *was* rest—her lap
was rest for me—who now is only fear
and quaking. I have been told, "Let go." Start
to separate myself. There will be time for this.
I came prepared the other day to call up
family ghosts, summoned to take a message
to the dead—a sister, gone at least a dozen years.
She's her father's last Kovarsky, Litvak to the core.
And she was fierce and hard to please and lovely.
Now she's an empty house, her head a room where
wildness roosts, black widows hang up webs.
How can I leave her?

            There is a forest
galloping faster than she can, over-taking her.
Green moss grows from her ceiling. This is a place
where no one stays. Enough that now I lay her
down to rest. Inscribe her in Your scroll at end,
an honored guest.

Pain Outside the Body

1

She used talcum on her face so that even her love for me did not show. When she died everything seemed so plain. She used to ask me what it was I was thinking. I could see her worry and would answer, *nothing*. And she would say, *no, there is something.*

2

I once saw a man fall overboard into the sea. The ship steamed away at thirty knots. This is not a great speed. And the horizon looked to be a perfect circle. I was always at the center. And when the man who fell overboard was saved, I thought about myself.

3

Her body was still warm. I spoke to her in a soft voice, not wanting to wake her. With my hand I smoothed a few stray hairs from her forehead that always used to bother her. This one time they stayed perfectly in place.

REASSURANCE

I draw a chair
beside your last bed
in your last room,
your face powdered and rouged
like a mask
whose mouth searches for joy
and questions despair.

You tell me
of the little girl
in a monkey's cap
who stood beside your bed last night.
You shuddered when ants
infested your pillow
and nested like lice upon your hands.
I'm sorry I didn't hear you
when you called out to me.

Your fingers flutter,
fly us to the oaken banister
your hand smoothed morning and evening.
Your eyes blink back
with Dad's name and mine.
Maybe tomorrow you'll remember us.
Maybe . . .

Is Past a haven from Present?
I could walk away,
leave you in questions without answers,
but I am your son,
a boy sitting beside you on a piano bench
and listening to love songs
I once thought only make-believe.

LIMITS

We defied time for a long time.
I would have kissed you as long as I could.

When you brought your wide-open love
neither of us thought of limits.

Maybe you knew the rules for the duration of happiness.
Maybe that was why you lied about your age.

I was so surprised that day in the hospital
when I saw your license—your only lie.

I still thought it was "till death do us part,"
but sometimes death takes only part of us at first.

If I had known I could have all those years
and then be forced to see you fade away,

how long I'd have to be alone,
while you looked on with vacant eyes,
grasping for words you used to know,

would I have taken the deal?

You were so funny, your slim legs so long,
your heart so near the surface,

how could I have resisted you?
I who now clean and mourn.

St. Tara

Behind the mask her eyes burn,
memory shredded like the Confetti Bible.

What day is today?
A minute later:
What day is today?

The dogs have eaten. Or have they?
Look for their bowls, smiling in the sink.

I have to go to the bank, she says.
I need to buy some money.

Knobs have grown teeth,
stalks have sharp edges,
dials tell lies.

The mail is full of danger.

I read her old poems to her.
That's good, she says.
Did I write that?
Are you sure?

Dearest blessed St. Tara of the Broken Memory,
whose brilliance once cast shadows on the moon,
who made a roomful laugh until they hurt,
now cries in confusion,
rages against herself,
cannot accept her loss.

Rest peacefully, my sweet,
enjoy the sun
and the food your weary lover
offers you in lieu of tears.

VISITING DEMENTIA

The weeping
at least
allows us someplace to be
and your room is defined.

It is what
keeps us to each other

the joining force—

for can you not feel what the sky
has wanted

its strong pull
at your drowsy will

tugging
that draws
your expression up into it.

Lately, I have noticed rains
Father, I have seen your eyes
clouded over

that look of yours
busy elsewhere

spotting angels.

When at last
they fully enter this air
for you

I will have almost nothing afterward—

I will lose that long term
of belonging
to illness.

LEANING IN

Leaning down and in
to approximate you.
How close can my face become?
I do not ask that
you wake up. That story
is never ending.
Still, as if to kiss your lids,
I purse my lips.

Burt Rashbaum

SUMMONING MY MOTHER

I can talk to you again
like I haven't been able to
in years.
You know my name
and recognize me.
You remember my birthday
and laugh at my jokes
and want to understand
my silence.

When did the music stop?
I hadn't noticed it gone.
Perhaps it's been a long long time,
but I think it's started up again;
faint, but clear.

Now, to look for you, I can
look into the depths of my own heart.
A bit of you is in the sky
and in the cool wind
and in spring's cleansing rain.

Hey Ma, we're going to have a baby!
Hey Ma, we're doing okay!
I even think the stars are shining again,
and though I'll miss you forever,
I think you've finally found your way
home,
back into my father's loving arms.

Ashley Pacholewski

Travel Plans

I have never existed in a world without you
And now, what should be celebrated—
New life growing—
Becomes a countdown clock to your new world
Away from me.

How eerie, to feel your own death—
Little legs and knees kicking away—
Seeing it give you delight in the
Growing end of earthy you.

I once heard death described as a birth—
A new awakening into a realm we can't conceptualize.
How do you explain the world to an unborn child?
How do you explain being unborn to a living soul
That's made their home, their family, their legacy
A migration into another un-conceptualized plane?

You've traveled from womb to world
And child to parent. From grandma back again to child.
Perhaps you recognize this transition will be the greatest—
Each move has been a fulfilling ride.

Maybe you're going back to the place
We all came from, and that otherworldly smile
Is a memory of your true home.

Send me a postcard.
My world without you—
Will be my own adventure.

SWEET AND BLUE

Barbara Hill

HYACINTHS

—after wcw

This is just to say
that I've taken six
of your blue hyacinths
to Louise at Piper Shores

I thought you wouldn't mind

She probably won't remember
who I am and she'll be distressed
but the hyacinths
will move us
beyond the moment
of failed memory

into the present
which is sweet
and blue
and lasts forever

Acknowledgments

"Alzheimer Definition" published in *Chest*, Volume 154, No. 2, 2018. Copyright © 2018 Herbert Woodward Martin.

"Brain Tangle" published in *Unique Poetry*, September 11, 2020. Copyright © 2020 Myra Ward Barra.

"Close Up" published in *Open to Interpretation: Fading Light*, 2013. Copyright © 2013 Yvonne Pearson.

"Earl Grey" published in *Word Doodles*, 1:1, Summer 2020; and in *Medical Literary Messenger*, Fall/Winter 2020. Copyright © 2020 Sandra Dreis.

"Sophie" published in *Waking up the Ducks*, Adastra Press, 1987. Copyright © 1987 Wally Swist.

"Bereft" published in *Distillery*, Volume XV, No. 1, July 2008. Copyright © 2008 Charlotte McCaffrey.

"They" published in *Editing Sky*, Texas Review Press/Texas A&M University Press Consortium, 1999; in *The Texas Review Special Poetry Issue*, Spring/Summer 2000; and in *Beyond Forgetting: Poetry and Prose about Alzheimer's Disease*, Kent State University Press, 2009. Copyright © 2009 David M. Parsons.

"On the Sunset, Eastbound" published in *Tell Her Yes*, The Poetry Box, 2022. Copyright © 2022 Ann Farley.

"Search Party" published in *Poetry*, March 2000; in *Kathleen Lynch Greatest Hits*, Pudding House Publications, 2002; and in *Hinge*, Black Zinnias Press, 2006. Copyright © 2006 Kathleen Lynch.

"Mind Erasure" published in *Beyond Words Literary Magazine*, October 2020. Copyright © 2020 Pamela Peté.

"Learned at Last Night's Lecture on Dementia" published in *Tar River Poetry*, Volume. 57, No. 2, Spring 2018. Copyright © 2018 Pam Baggett.

"Alzheimer's for Beginners" published in *The Works, Block Island's Arts Magazine*, September 1992. Copyright © 1992 Nancy Walker Greenaway.

"Swimming in the Rain" published in Willawaw Review, Issue 7, Fall 2019; and in *Stealing Flowers from the Neighbors*, Kelsay Press, 2021. Copyright © 2021 Sherri H. Levine.

Many thanks to Lisa Hendron for her kind and generous assistance with proofreading.

CONTRIBUTORS

AUSTIN ALEXIS is the author of *Privacy Issues* (Broadside Lotus Press) and two chapbooks. He hopes that his poem "Dementia Intrigue" conveys how gradual and mysterious the progression of the illness was for both his mother and her loved ones.

PAM BAGGETT found caring for her mother to be one of the most profoundly beautiful and challenging experiences of her life. Throughout her mother's eleven-year decline, there was deep grief in the slow, inexorable loss of a parent and joy in finding acceptance as her mother became more like a delightful child. Pam is author of *Wild Horses* (Main Street Rag, 2018).

MARSHA BARBER was her mother's caregiver for five years until her mother died in 2021. Marsha's fourth poetry book, *Kaddish for My Mother*, will be published in 2022. She is on faculty at Toronto Metropolitan University and a member of the League of Canadian Poets.
  • m2barber@ryerson.ca

WALTER BARGEN spent six years taking care of his mother, Anna Franziska Bargen, as she passed through and beyond dementia. He recorded their experience in the book *My Other Mother's Red Mercedes* (Lamar University Literary Press, 2018). The two poems that appear in *Storms of the Inland Sea* first appeared in the above-mentioned book.

MYRA WARD BARRA is a poet, artist, and medical business owner. She composes work from her experience with people in all stages of life. Her work has been recognized through national and state poetry associations. She is on the board of Writers Anonymous and is a past board member of the Alabama State Poetry Society.

CHARLES BECKER is a retired speech pathologist who worked with children in educational settings. He has written many poems about favorite family members. Charles's poem "At 97" chronicles his mother's serious short-term memory problems which began at age 95. Throughout her experience of dementia, however, she never lost her sense of humor.

A physician and poet, RICHARD M. BERLIN is the author of four poetry collections, and his poetry has been published in *Psychiatric Times* every month since 1997. He is an experienced nursing home psychiatrist, serves on the faculty of University of Massachusetts Medical School, and practices in the Berkshire hills of western Massachusetts.
  • www.richardmberlin.com

In 1979 ALAN BERN's wife delivered a healthy child after having a brain bleed that left her permanently brain-damaged. In 1983 she died without understanding that she had had a child. "Leaning In" is one fixed memory from her time in a coma. Retired children's librarian, performer, and published photographer, Alan has awards for his poems and stories.

- www.linesandfaces.com

SANDRA BERRIS found solace in writing poetry to capture the unanticipated and inescapable challenges of caregiving for elderly parents. Her poems balance the loss and heartbreak of dementia with reflection, whimsy, and humor. Her collection *Ash on Wind* was published by Muse Ink Press in 2017.

- www.sandraberris.com

JEFF BURT lives in Santa Cruz County, California, with his wife. He works in mental health. During his father-in-law's battle with multiple system atrophy, Jeff learned the value of silence, to wait for the hesitant speech of his father-in-law so that he could participate in family conversation, and how to rub feeling back into feet.

- www.jeff-burt.com

DANE CERVINE's books include *The World Is God's Language* (Sixteen Rivers Press) and *Earth Is a Fickle Dancer* (Main Street Rag). Poems in this anthology originate from his former experience working in long-term care. Dane lives in Santa Cruz, California, where he maintains a small therapy practice.

- danecervine.typepad.com

MARION DEUTSCHE COHEN is the author of thirty-two books of poetry and memoir, including *Dirty Details: The Days and Nights of a Well Spouse* (Temple University Press) and *Still the End: Memoirs of a Nursing Home Wife* (Unlimited Publishing). She was a well-spouse for twenty-six years when her late husband contended with multiple sclerosis.

- marioncohen.net

JIM COKAS is an artist whose work involves visual imagery as well as poetry. His father, George, suffered from Alzheimer's for over eighteen years. Jim spent a great deal of time trying to bring George some peace and pleasure while writing poems to process and document their time together.

- www.jimcokas.com

JOY COLTER lives in Rock Hill, South Carolina. Poetry was her emotional outlet as she watched her mother, Corrie, be consumed by Alzheimer's dementia. Balancing being a caring daughter versus a detached caregiver was difficult but necessary to weather the chaos that came with the disease, as alluded to in the poem "Cleaning House."

JOHN DAVIS lives on an island in the Salish Sea and is the author of *Gigs* and *The Reservist*. Caring for his father was an ongoing challenge while witnessing cognitive and physical skills diminish from a man who had once been very alert and active and enjoyed the vitality of life.

ALBERT DEGENOVA endured with his mother the existential loss that Alzheimer's delivers. He did not write poems to chronicle her disease but as witness to the horrors that he and his siblings experienced as their mother deteriorated. DeGenova is an award-winning poet and teacher. He is also the founder/editor of *After Hours*, a journal of Chicago writing and art.
- albertdegenova.com

SANDRA DREIS writes prose and poetry. Her Young Adult novel, *The Ecowarriors—The Bluffs of Baraboo*, received a Silver Nautilus Award in 2016. Her poetry can be found in *Flying South, Poetry in Plain Sight*, and *The Main Street Rag*. Sandra was privileged to be primary caregiver for her mother, Harriet, who passed away from Alzheimer's in 2019, demonstrating a zest for life for ninety-four years.

KELLY DUMAR is a poet, playwright, and workshop facilitator from Boston. She's the author of three poetry chapbooks, and her poems, prose, and photos are published in many literary journals. Kelly serves on the board of the Transformative Language Arts Network and produces the Monthly Open Mic for the *Journal of Expressive Writing*.
- www.kellydumar.com/blog

JO ANGELA EDWINS grew up on the border between Georgia and South Carolina and now lives in Florence, South Carolina, where she serves as poet laureate of the Pee Dee region of South Carolina. Her father, Joe, a former housing contractor and WWII veteran, passed away in January 2013 at age 85 after suffering for several years from vascular dementia and heart failure.
- joangelaedwins.wordpress.com

CARRIE ROSE EVON worked for two years as a caregiver at a small assisted living facility. This experience inspired her to write poetry for the residents' families. Carrie's poem in this collection is dedicated to Steve and to Grampa Henry Kakazu, who passed away from dementia-related complications in 2020.
- carrieroseevon.wixsite.com/about

"Caregiving isn't a job, it's a relationship," says ANN FARLEY, caregiver and poet from Beaverton, Oregon. "When spending time with a person who has dementia, slow down, or come to a complete stop, to give the person a chance to focus and connect. Be open to a magical moment of connection, even in a traffic jam."

- www.annfarleypoetry.com

ZOE FITZGERALD-BECKETT lives in the Maine countryside. Her work has been published in *Dreamers, The Healing Muse, The Sun, ZestMaine*, and *Sage Woman*. Her poetry often reflects an empathy with the suffering of others. "Destination Unknown" was written as a form of witness to a dear friend's struggle and heartbreak over her husband's experience of and eventual death from dementia.

- zoefitzgeraldbeckett@gmail.com

ALICE FRIMAN's seventh book of poetry is *Blood Weather* (LSU Press). She says, "Although my mother didn't succumb to dementia until the end at 96, the heartbreak of caring for her in her last six years was that she slowly retreated into herself, becoming a stone. The hardest years of my life."

- www.alicefrimanpoet.com

LESLIE GERBER was born in Brooklyn in 1943 and graduated from Brooklyn College. He began writing poetry in 1999 and was greatly encouraged by his wife, a full-time professional writer. During her decade of decline into dementia, he wrote many poems about their experiences, published after she died as *Losing Tara*.

- www.lesliegerber.net

LENORA RAIN-LEE GOOD lives by the Columbia River in Kennewick, Washington. Though not a caregiver in the traditional sense of the word, she has friends and family of choice who are in various stages of dementia. On viewing the movie *Poetry* the first time, it all came together in her poem "Saving against Alzheimer's."

- coffeebreakescapes.com

TZIVIA GOVER began writing poetry at age 10 and has relied on writing to help her make sense of the ineffable experiences of life, love, and loss ever since. She has written extensively about her lifelong friendship with her mother, including the poem featured here from their last chapter together. Tzivia is also a certified professional dreamworker.

- tziviagover.com

NANCY WALKER GREENAWAY provided support for her husband in his care for his mother. A teacher and medical center administrator, Nancy wrote poetry about her experience with her mother-in-law's ever-more-debilitating Alzheimer's. Writing helped her to understand emotions and events more fully and to cope more patiently.

Like so many, PENNY HACKETT-EVANS struggled with the decision to put her mother into a memory care unit when she realized she could not care for her on her own. Penny feels indebted to the care that her mother was given by minimum wage-earning women who treated her mother with great dignity.

VANESSA HALEY's poem addresses losing both parents simultaneously. While her mother was in "home-hospice" dying of cancer, her father began showing signs of dementia, which at first were mistaken for stress-related expressions of longstanding personality traits. Vanessa practices psychotherapy in Delaware.

THERESE HALSCHEID's father suffered brain damage during heart surgery when she was 14. Having a father with active dementia was traumatic, which resulted in her starving herself. This was 1973, when words like Alzheimer's and anorexia were unknown. Her poems from her book *Frozen Latitudes* offer a glimpse into their paired illness. She and her mother cared for him for thirty years.
  • www.theresehalscheid.com

JIM HANLEN has published over seventy poems. He has poems printed recently in *Rattle, Cirque, Earth's Daughters*, and *13 Chairs*. He retired from teaching in Washington and lives in Anchorage, Alaska.

PAULETTA HANSEL's book, *Palindrome*, about caring for her mother, Larnie Lewis Hansel, won Berea College's Weatherford Award. She leads writing workshops in support of caregivers for the organizations 55 North and the Giving Voice Foundation, which has published a writing journal for caregivers, *Caring in Our Own Words*. Pauletta was Cincinnati's first poet laureate.
  • paulettahansel.wordpress.com

MARC HARSHMAN's *Woman in Red Anorak*, published in 2018, was winner of the Blue Lynx Poetry Prize. His fourteenth children's book, *Fallingwater…*, co-authored with Anna Smucker, was published by Roaring Brook/Macmillan in 2017 and named an Amazon Book of the Month. He is also co-winner of the 2019 Allen Ginsberg Poetry Award. In 2012 he was appointed seventh poet laureate of West Virginia.

BARBARA HILL is a poet and interfaith minister from Stonington, Connecticut. Her book, *A Few Sharp and Glamorous Words*, was published in 2019. She has worked as a caregiver for family members and others with dementia. Her poem "Hyacinths" expresses both the distress of memory loss and the welcome relief of beauty in the present moment.

JACK HITCHNER's poetry appeared in *Seasons and Shadows, Pieces of Life Between Latitudes*, and *Like Snow Upon Green*. His father, a victim of Alzheimer's, is reflected in some of his poetry.
- jack.t.hitchner@gmail.com

At age 79, Milton Henry Hollander, a World War II veteran and later a New Jersey pediatrician, as well as the father of poet ANDREA HOLLANDER, was diagnosed with Alzheimer's. Andrea lived in Arkansas and could visit only several times a year. Until his death at 91, his steadfast wife, Evelyn, took care of him at home.
- www.andreahollander.net

PAUL HOSTOVSKY's Aunt Edie, the subject of his two poems in this anthology, currently resides in the Hannah B. Shaw Home in Middleborough, Massachusetts. As her dementia has progressed, his conversations with her have been heartbreaking, hilarious, intriguing, revelatory, and inspiring. Paul's latest book of poetry is *Mostly* (FutureCycle Press, 2021).
- paulhostovsky.com

While HOLLY J. HUGHES wasn't the primary caregiver for her mother, she stepped in when she could to give her father a break, turning to her Buddhist practice and poetry to help navigate and honor the moments of grace. She's the editor of *Beyond Forgetting: Poetry and Prose about Alzheimer's Disease*, and five other books, most recently, *Hold Fast*.
- www.hollyjhughes.com

THERESA HUPP provided long-distance support to her maternal grandmother and then her mother as they battled Alzheimer's over three decades. Theresa has written five historical novels about settling the American West, as well as two contemporary novels published under a pseudonym. She has won awards for her poetry, short stories, and novels.
- www.theresahuppauthor.com

RICK KEMPA's poem "Prayer for My Mother" honors the memory of his dear mom, Irene, who for two precious years, until her needs grew too great, lived with his family and him. Irene was claimed by Alzheimer's disease in 2011. The poem first appeared in *Passager*.
- www.rickkempa.com

CLAIRE KEYES's husband, Jay Moore, was undergoing the final stages of Parkinson's disease when she wrote her poems. He had mild dementia. While this was extremely sad, it was also a period of searching and spirituality. Did he know what was happening? Possibly. Claire's books of poetry include *The Question of Rapture* and *What Diamonds Can Do*.

PATRICIA LAPIDUS has published poems in anthologies and literary journals. Her books include a health memoir and a novel about family healing. When Patricia's husband's dementia became advanced, she visited him at the nursing home where he lived for two years. She encouraged him to relearn the piano and supplemented the sweet memories he'd lost.
  • patricialapidus.com

SHERRI H. LEVINE lives in Portland, Oregon. Her full-length poetry collection, *Stealing Flowers from the Neighbors*, was released in September 2021. Her poem "Swimming in the Rain" is about taking her mother swimming as a break from the daily struggles of her Alzheimer's disease. Levine felt immense joy and relief watching her swim, smile, and laugh.
  • sherrilevine.com

IRIS LITT is the author of three books/chapbooks of poems and has had poems and short stories in many magazines, including *Confrontation, Saturday Evening Post, Mud Season Review, London Magazine,* and *Travelers' Tales*. She has taught creative writing as adjunct at SUNY/Ulster, Bard College, and Writers in the Mountain. She has also taught at the New York Public Library and the Brooklyn Public Library. She lives in Woodstock, New York.

JOEL LONG's book *Winged Insects* won the White Pine Press Poetry Prize. *Lessons in Disappearance* (2012) and *Knowing Time by Light* (2010) were published by Blaine Creek Press. His chapbooks, *Chopin's Preludes* and *Saffron Beneath Every Frost* were published by Elik Press. He lives in Salt Lake City where he teaches English and creative writing at Rowland Hall-St. Mark's.

KATHLEEN LYNCH's first book, *Hinge,* won The Black Zinnias Award and her second, *Lucky Witness*, was published by Blue Light Press in 2019. Her poetry, prose, and essays have appeared in many anthologies and journals. "Search Party" is based on an actual event when Jack Lloyd wandered off, triggering a citywide search by scores of people, including Kathleen.

MARJORIE MADDOX has published fourteen collections of poetry, including the ekphrastic collaboration *Heart Speaks, Is Spoken For,* with two forthcoming; four children's books; and a story collection. A university professor, she also has cared for her mother and father-in-law in the depths of dementia, the focus of her newest manuscript, which includes poems published in *JAMA* and *Ars Medica*.
  • www.marjoriemaddox.com

EILEEN MALONE is a widely published poet and fiction writer who has been featured in poetry journals and readings nationally and internationally. Her writing awards for her poetry and stories include four

nominations for Pushcart Prizes. She is a mental health activist (NAMI) and this poem came from a caretaker of an elderly parent with dementia.
• www.eileenmalone.us

HERBERT WOODWARD MARTIN and Betty McAfee met in the late 1970s. Soon after, she became his mother-in-law, and their relationship was a happy and connected one. After Betty's Alzheimer's diagnosis, he became her caregiver. They became inseparable, going to rehearsals, daycare, and lunches. At that time, he wrote the Alzheimer poems, including "Alzheimer Definition."
• hmartin1@udayton.edu

CHARLOTTE MCCAFFREY is a writer who resides in the San Francisco Bay Area. When her father was diagnosed with dementia and went into hospice, she advocated and helped care for him. The experience gave her a deep appreciation for his other devoted caregivers and strengthened her relationship with her father, even as he was slipping away.
• cmcc25@comcast.net

MARIANA MCDONALD is a poet, writer, scientist, and activist. Her late husband, Ramón Feliciano, was diagnosed with early-onset Alzheimer's disease, which took his life after nine years. Mcdonald cared for her husband while she raised their children, ages three and eight at the time of his diagnosis, and worked as a public health professional.

ROBIN MICHEL's writing has appeared online or in print in many journals, and she is the editor of *How to Begin: Poems, Prompts, Tips and Writing Exercises* from the Fresh Ink Poetry Collective (Raven & Wren Press, 2020). Her poem "In Mid-Afternoon," written from her mother's point of view, recounts an actual conversation the two of them shared.
• www.robinmichelwriter.com

FELICIA MITCHELL turned to poetry, a lifelong habit, to navigate her caregiving experience with her mother, Audrey. While having her mother nearby during her last years was a joy, the dementia journey had its challenges. These challenges could include a simple outing to a coffee shop or the ripple effect on Mitchell's own self-image and family life.
• www.feliciamitchell.net

PAMELA A. MITCHELL's career of caregiving spans forty-five years as a registered nurse. Her chapbook, *Finding Lost Pond* (Finishing Line Press, April 2021), documents her work and what sustained her. "Roommates" is the story of her father battling dementia in his final year. Despite its challenges, she feels blessed to have assisted in his care.
• pammitchelldotblog.wordpress.com

In 2008 TARA MOGHADAM returned to her native Minnesota to be near her aging parents. It soon became apparent that her father was becoming incapacitated with dementia. The following seven years were ones of heartbreak, caregiving, and love as she watched her father disappear from the world he had worked so hard to create.

• www.islandsoulstudios.com

JUDITH H. MONTGOMERY was a primary (and simultaneous) caregiver for her mother (Alzheimer's) and her father (congestive heart failure), eliciting moments of despair, anxiety, and the purest love. Her first collection, *Passion*, received the Oregon Book Award. Her most recent collection, *Mercy* (2019), which traced her and her husband's cancer journey, won the Wolf Ridge Press Narrative/Poetic Medicine Chapbook Award.

TIM J. MYERS is a writer, storyteller, songwriter, visual artist, and senior lecturer at Santa Clara University in Silicon Valley. He creates work for all ages. His university office used to be around the corner from an Alzheimer's day center, and that experience inspired this poem as well as others.

• www.timmyersstorysong.com

ASHLEY PACHOLEWSKI teaches English and writes poetry as a creative outlet. She has published in Cleveland's *Hessler Street Fair Poetry Anthology*, 2015 and 2018, and Ohio Poetry Day Association's *Best of the Best 2020*. Ashley helped care for her grandmother Betty Pace after her grandfather's passing and was thankful for the time together, ice cream sundaes, and summer weather.

DAVID M. PARSONS, 2011 Texas Poet Laureate, is recipient of an NEH Dante Fellowship to SUNY, the French-American Legation Poetry Prize, TCU's Baskerville Publisher's Prize, and is an inductee into The Texas Institute of Letters. His latest book is *Reaching For Longer Water*. His father-in-law, Harry Dazey, gave him the title for his poem "They" as that was the word he used to describe his illness.

• daveparsonspoetry.com

YVONNE PEARSON helped to care for her mother for the approximately five years she lived with Alzheimer's disease. Her poem is about the hardest part of that experience—watching her mother slowly disappear so that it seemed she was gone before she was gone. Yvonne is a poet and children's author who has two new picture books coming soon.

• yvonnepearson.com

ELLEN PECKHAM honored a promise to care for her husband, Anson, as long as she possibly could in their home. As the responsibility increased and it became impossible for her to go to her art studio, poetry became

her dominant form used to express emotion, the gut pain, and functional desertion, guiltless but searing.
- www.ellenpeckham.com

PAMELA PETÉ is a US veteran, poet, speaker, and business owner. She recently received her MFA in Creative Writing in Performing Arts. She is blessed to assist in the care of her sister with dementia. This heart-wrenching experience is spilling onto the page through her poems. Her motto is "Wake-up on Purpose—Your Masterful Purpose!"
- www.masterfulpurpose.com

YVONNE POSTELLE wrote *After Beauty* as a memorial to her husband, Jack Peary. Drawn from journals and memories of her caregiving years, these poems became her means to process loss while simultaneously celebrating their nineteen years together. She still takes comfort from this memorial volume, which won first prize as the best self-published book of poetry, Writer's Digest, 2012.
- postelley@gmail.com

WANDA S. PRAISNER, her husband's caregiver for five devastating years, lost part of herself along the way. Two decisions that had to be made: to find part-time help when he could no longer be left alone; to take him to a nursing home when she could no longer care for him. More devastating: living without him.

BURT RASHBAUM's father died young from heart disease. His mother soon contracted early-onset Alzheimer's. As her main caregiver, he watched her slow and sad descent over the course of eight years. Upon her death, this poem was written with the hope that, as it states, she was in his father's loving arms again.

J. E. ROBINSON has had his work appear widely. The poem "Nursing Home" reflects his fear of family abandonment, which living with schizophrenia requires him to face. He teaches history at the University of Health Sciences and Pharmacy in St. Louis.

SUSAN RONEY-O'BRIEN's first job was in a nursing home housing elders suffering from dementia. Some families came every week; others chose not to. "She doesn't know me" was a common excuse. Although "Changeling" uses her mother as the main character, it was her aunt who lived with Alzheimer's. The Irish connection is true.

MARJORIE STAMM ROSENFELD is a former Southern Methodist University Press editor, SMU English instructor, and US Navy analyst who has done poetry therapy with forensic patients. She created three websites to commemorate perished Jewish communities in eastern Europe. Her work has appeared in numerous journals and anthologies. Her chapbook, *Fringing the Garments*, was published in 2013 by Pecan Grove Press, St. Mary's University.

Poet-writer MARY HARWELL SAYLER has primary care for a loved one whose puns still make her laugh and prayers heal. Eventually an actual dog strayed into her yard, determined to stay. While home and church activities abound, Mary is also active on social media, her blogs, and website with links to resources for other poets and writers.
  • maryharwellsayler.wordpress.com

MARY ELLEN SHAUGHAN embarked on a new path after retirement: she began working with seniors, helping them to remain in the comfort and familiarity of their homes as long as possible. She was unprepared to meet and grow to love so many extraordinary people who were affected by dementia. Find more of her poetry in her book *Home Grown*.

MATTHEW SISSON's poetry has appeared in journals ranging from the *Harvard Review Online* to *JAMA: The Journal of the American Medical Association*. He has been nominated for a Pushcart Prize and read his work on NPR's *On Point with Tom Ashbrook*. His first book, *Please, Call Me Moby*, was published by Pecan Grove Press, St. Mary's University, San Antonio, Texas.

PAUL SOHAR escaped Soviet-occupied Hungary in 1956 for the US where he got a BA in philosophy and a day job in chemistry. At night, he wrote in every genre, including seventeen volumes of translations. His own poetry: *Homing Poems* (Iniquity Press), *The Wayward Orchard* (Wordrunner Press Prize winner), and *In Sun's Shadow* (Ragged Sky Press, 2020).
  • sohar.paul@gmail.com

MARIAN BROWN ST ONGE retired from Boston College, where she was director of international programs, taught French, and directed the women's studies program. The recipient of several fellowships and awards, her publications include poems and articles on cultural issues. St Onge's interest in people suffering from dementia went back to her college years when she worked with elderly women in a psychiatric hospital. She died on August 18, 2021.

MARGARET STAWOWY was her mother's caregiver for more than five years. Her mother lacked financial resources, so when her dementia became aggressive and violent, it proved quite difficult to cobble together needed care within the limits of a piecemeal system. She misses her mother a lot.
  • margaretstawowy.weebly.com

Poet and memoir artist DOREEN STOCK of Fairfax, California, recently launched *Bye Bye Blackbird* (The Poetry Box, April 2021), a chapbook of poems about her mother's last days. "The Poem Geronimo," from this collection, touches upon the dementia resulting from chronic bladder infections.
 • doreenstock.com

WALLY SWIST's poem "Sophie" originates from his work as a caregiver in a Level IV rest home in Monson, Massachusetts, in the early 1980s. His books include *Evanescence: Selected Poems* (2020), *A Writer's Statements on Beauty: New & Selected Essays & Reviews* (2021), and *Taking Residence* (2021), all with Shanti Arts.

SUSAN TERRIS is the author of seven books of poetry, seventeen chapbooks, three artist's books, and one play. Journals include *The Southern Review, Georgia Review, Prairie Schooner,* and *Ploughshares.* She has had poems published both in *Pushcart Prize* and in *Best American Poetry.* She provided short-term care for her mother-in-law with Alzheimer's and then eleven years as her husband's mind was ravaged by it.
 • www.susanterris.com

CAROL TYX wrote these poems while assisting with caregiving after her mother, Katie, broke her pelvis. She had already been experiencing Alzheimer's, but Carol found it fascinating (and heartbreaking) to observe the way her mother's mind shifted into a different gear after her fall. Writing poems helped Carol appreciate the humor and quirkiness of this stage of her mother's life.

TONY VICK has been incarcerated for twenty-five years. He writes about the emotions associated with confinement. His poetry speaks to the struggles that many elderly face in prison and to the worries those confined have about elderly loved ones.

KAREN VILLESVIK's mother had both pseudo and vascular dementia, as well as COPD and CHF. As Karen watched the changes in personality and the decline of an outgoing and creative intellect, she wrote poems to relieve her anguish. Being at her mother's side when she transitioned and passed has given Karen the courage to begin to share her poetry.

MICHAEL WATERS watched his mother deepen into her dementia as she moved through anxiety, paranoia, and knife-wielding anger to become, at 93, the American stereotype of the sweet and dotty little old lady. His book *Caw* (2020) contains a sequence of poems about aging, dementia, and caregiving.
 • www.michael-waters.com

MICHELE WOLF cared for her mother as her dementia progressed and she needed a daily home health aide, then twenty-four-hour supervision, first in an assisted living facility and later in a nursing home, where she died at age 79. Michele is the author of *Immersion, Conversations During Sleep* (Anhinga Prize for Poetry), and *The Keeper of Light*.

- www.michelewolf.com

JOSEPH ZACCARDI took care of his mother for the last ten years of her life, the last three in a nursing home, which for him was a gift. She would often say, "I'm sorry, Joey, to put you through this," and he'd tell her, "Mom you gave birth to me, loved me, and took care of me; I love taking care of you."

- www.josephzaccardi.com

ANDRENA ZAWINSKI's poetry is lauded for lyricism, form, spirituality, and social concern. Her poem "The Way It Is" reflects a coming to terms with her mother-in-law's life in a care facility once she became a danger to herself and others. Zawinski has authored four poetry books: *Born Under the Influence, Landings, Something About*, and *Traveling in Reflected Light*, as well as a collection of stories.

Shanti Arts

Nature ▪ Art ▪ Spirit

Please visit us online
to browse our entire book catalog,
including poetry collections and fiction,
books on travel, nature, healing, art,
photography, and more.

Also take a look at our highly regarded art
and literary journal, *Still Point Arts Quarterly*,
which may be downloaded for free.

www.shantiarts.com

CPSIA information can be obtained
at www.ICGtesting.com
Printed in the USA
LVHW082028261022
731670LV00026B/389